D0277204

QUEEN OF CRAFTS

THE MODERN GIRLS' GUIDE TO
Knitting, Sewing, Quilting, Baking,
Preserving and Kitchen Gardening

JAZZ DOMINO HOLLY

PENGUIN
FIG TREE

AN IMPRINT OF PENGUIN BOOKS

FIG TREE

Published by the Penguin Group
Penguin Books Ltd, 80 Strand, London WC2R 0RL, England
Penguin Group (USA) Inc., 375 Hudson Street, New York, New York 10014, USA
Penguin Group (Canada), 90 Eglinton Avenue East, Suite 700, Toronto, Ontario, Canada M4P 2Y3
(a division of Pearson Penguin Canada Inc.)
Penguin Ireland, 25 St Stephen's Green, Dublin 2, Ireland (a division of Penguin Books Ltd)
Penguin Group (Australia), 250 Camberwell Road,Camberwell, Victoria 3124, Australia
(a division of Pearson Australia Group Pty Ltd)
Penguin Books India Pvt Ltd, 11 Community Centre,
Panchsheel Park, New Delhi – 110 017, India
Penguin Group (NZ), 67 Apollo Drive, Rosedale, Auckland 0632, New Zealand
(a division of Pearson New Zealand Ltd)
Penguin Books (South Africa) (Pty) Ltd, 24 Sturdee Avenue,
Rosebank, Johannesburg 2196, South Africa

Penguin Books Ltd, Registered Offices: 80 Strand, London WC2R 0RL, England

www.penguin.com

First published 2011
1

Design and Art Direction by & SMITH
Illustrations by & SMITH
Typeset by & SMITH
Set in Akkurat , Light 8pt on 10.5pt
Printed and bound by Firmengruppe APPL, aprint

A CIP catalogue record for this book is available from the British Library

HARDBACK ISBN: 978–1–905–49075–2

MIX
Paper from
responsible sources
FSC™ C018179

To my grandmother Frances,
who always needles me into place

A special thank you must be made to Rachel Rayner for planting the
seed of the idea for this book and then helping it to grow by introducing
me to Rowan Lawton, my agent, without whose guidance none of this
would have been possible. But I also owe huge gratitude to all the team
at Fig Tree for taking a chance on me, most especially the brilliant and
hugely talented Jenny Lord, who has been not only my editor but also
crafts comrade in arms.

Many, many thanks too to all those who have passed on their
knowledge to me over the years, but especially to Aileen, Penny, Val
and Jan, who have always helped generously and without hesitation,
and, of course, to Rupert for teaching me how to knit! I would also
like to thank my friends and family for putting up with me, especially
Mum and Patrick for letting me and my stash take over their house
and giving me a place to rest my head and a room to write in. Also
to Grandpa Tom for always saying yes to dog-sitting Punky, and to
Lola, who has always been my go-to girl for advice. And, of course,
to Frances, my grandmother, whose help has been immeasurable
and to whom the book is dedicated. A thank you and a kiss goes out
to Brian, who has not only helped realize my dream designs but has
also never failed to be a constant source of strength through this
process. And, of course, to my girlies: Emmy, Kate and Birdy.

Last, but by no means least, I want to say a massive thank you to all
Shoreditch Sisters members both past and present, who have always
inspired and impressed me. Go girls!

INTRODUCTI

It's official: crafts are cool again. The ultimate comeback kid of the new millennium, crafting has won a new-found respect – knitting has been dubbed the new rock'n'roll and even cross-stitch has got radical. But apart from its emerging street cred, the best thing about crafting is that literally anyone can do it, even those who think themselves all fingers and thumbs. No matter what crafting skills you may or may not already possess, just remember that we all have the ability to create.

CRAFTING A NEW GENERATION

Today, a new generation of crafters are busy shaking up stereotypes by putting a fresh spin on old traditions and casting aside out-of-date notions of craft as just a hobby for grannies or housewives.

Activities once considered old-fashioned, like jam making, quilting and knitting, have now been revived and reinvigorated as exciting and creative outlets for self-expression among the hip and happening. And it's a sign of the times we live in: crafting is the perfect antidote to cookie-cutter mass production, and gives us a means of expressing not only our individuality but also our originality in a handmade rebellion against passive consumption.

Growing awareness of environmentalism and the need to recycle has also helped contribute to the rise in crafting's popularity, by bringing to light the ways in which DIY can revolutionize the way we live. Long gone are the days of frugal necessity – fortunately, unlike many generations of resourceful men and women before us, we no longer have to knit our own jumpers, patch our own quilts or darn our own socks.

ON

Technological advancements in this digital age have also been a motivating factor in the explosion of a worldwide craft movement.

But learning these skills is a fun and satisfying process that can also empower you with a sense of creative accomplishment and control. Learning to craft gives you a chance to have a say in shaping your world, literally putting the power back into the hands of the people. And for many, the handmade has now become a lifestyle choice, an attempt to oppose sweatshop labour practices and forge an independent micro-economy through the buying and selling of handmade goods. The online phenomenon Etsy.com (think eBay but for crafts) has provided a global platform for this kind of exchange, allowing people the opportunity to turn their talents into day jobs. Now, this may all sound a bit serious to some or might even be a bit too socks and sandals for others, but believe me, this is exciting stuff. Modern-day crafting has detonated with dynamite force all over the world.

Technological advancements in this digital age have also been a motivating factor in the explosion of a worldwide craft movement. Being able to reach out to each other virtually through websites, blogs, online forums and social networking sites like Ravelry.com (aka facebook for knitters) has helped to connect crafters all over the world like never before. The internet has become a hotbed of creativity, as for the first time in history those who like to craft have the world's attention as they upload and download projects and share inspiration and ideas at the click of a button.

Yet ironically, this over-reliance on modern technology has also left many nostalgic for good old-fashioned face-to-face communication, and back-to-basics connections are now being rediscovered through crafting clubs. Ever since Debbie Stoller (of *Bust* magazine fame) launched the first Stitch 'n Bitch group in New York in 1999, group crafting has taken off across the globe. People are once again getting together to craft in public, joining sewing groups, quilting clubs, knitting circles, Women's Institute groups and attending craft fairs to share ideas and opportunities as well as trade tips, techniques, patterns and projects.

A movement called Craftivism has even taken things one step further, aiming to change attitudes using crafts (craft plus activism – get it?). And that's one of the best things about participating in crafts: there are so many ways to help keep heritage alive and kicking. Today, crafting is as modern as tomorrow.

While I've certainly been riding the crest of the new craft wave for some time, kicking up all sorts of creative storms with my WI high jinks and other crafty exploits, this get-your-hands-dirty creativity is nothing new to me.

GROWING UP AGAINST THE GRAIN

I come from a long line of mavericks and mischief makers (my grandfather is still probably one of the naughtiest people I know) who have dared to both think and live outside the box – especially my dad, Joe Strummer, front man of London punk band The Clash.

With a punk rocker for a dad, the last thing people expect you to do is take up knitting and start your own chapter of the Women's Institute. You could call it teenage rebellion but, truth be told, the do-it-yourself spirit underpinning the emerging craft movement has been ingrained in me since birth. For as long as I can remember, our household paid homage to my and my sister's handiwork. Every doodle or flick of paint became to our parents a treasured token of our burgeoning creative talents – so much so that we were even allowed to scribble on the walls. In fact, making a mess was positively encouraged and our toys never had to be put away at the end of the day. Any visitors who stopped by the house for a cup of tea had to tiptoe through a crazy-paving debris of games, toys and makeshift camps.

Both our parents had been part of the London squatting scene during the late 70s, a lifestyle where turning trash into treasure was a part of everyday life. And our dad was rarely seen leaving the house without his trademark black Sharpie pen and a roll of Gaffa tape, as he never knew when he might want to mend a broken ghetto blaster or patch up and personalize a beat-up guitar.

Growing up in West London's Ladbroke Grove during the 80s, with its vibrant and lively atmosphere – a perfect clash of culture, music, art and fashion – we had the good fortune to know and live alongside a colourful variety of people, all of whom left their creative imprints on my memory. Traditionally, craft skills have been passed down through generations and although, sadly, this has become outmoded in recent years, I have been lucky enough that my friends and family have provided me with boundless sources of inspiration and the motivation to make and create.

Hands down, my greatest crafting icon of all time was my great-grandmother Dolly, the most prolific crafter in our family, and my fascination with making things began with her.

Hands down, my greatest crafting icon of all time was my great-grandmother Dolly, the most prolific crafter in our family, and my fascination with making things began with her. A woman of many talents, she was, at various times, a model, a dancer, a stuntwoman, a single mother, a working mother and – the icing on the cake – a multi-skilled craftswoman too. I remember as a child being in awe of her giant rainbow-hued crocheted blankets and the psychedelic tapestry cushions that cluttered the cosy front room where she taught me my first knit stitches. She had even handmade my grandmother's wedding gown – a big meringue-shaped fantasy with lashings of taffeta and lace, the stuff of fairy tales. My grandmother, in turn, learnt only a handful of these skills, mostly patchwork and cooking.

She was a swinging 60s playgirl who later became a hippy, sprouting seedlings under the kitchen sink in Ibiza (a habit I have also come to embrace, see p. 154). My own mother, unfortunately, inherited none of these talents, or, more likely perhaps, she lacked the inclination. She was a real Chelsea girl, a King's Road punk of the 70s who always had her finger on the pulse and was more interested in the fashion of her heyday. Nicknamed Punkerella, she was a menace in a mini skirt with her buzzed-up and back-combed hair and her one and only (albeit utterly impressive) claim to crafting fame was stitching my dad a cowboy shirt from scratch.

When it comes to crafting, I have taken after my grandmother more than my mother, and over the years I have tried my hand at almost everything going: knitting, sewing, embroidery, baking, gardening – you name it, you can bet I've tried it. But my favourite crafty moments have always revolved around friends. Getting together before a night out on the town, most teenagers would have been pulling out the hooch but I used to pull out the neon fabric paint and get my mates to hand-stencil slogans on to our rave T-shirts. Much like my parents used to do back in the day with their own DIY punk T-shirts, which both my little sis and I still have and wear today.

Most of my crafting skills were picked up either through sheer enthusiasm or by experimentation. Making things up as I go along has always been an act of rebellion, as I love the shambolic nature of DIY and the radical potential and possibilities it has to offer not only the maker but the world. When you make something by hand, it becomes ingrained with personal significance and value so you are less likely to throw it away. This is the true essence of the handmade – creating something useful or beautiful out of miscellaneous materials and relishing the process as much as the end product. For me, learning to craft is an extension of this ethos, and I taught myself to not only knit, stitch and bake my way through the handmade tradition but also embrace it, in all its wonky-round-the-edges and uneven stitchery.

When you make something by hand, it becomes ingrained with personal significance and value so you are less likely to throw it away. This is the true essence of the handmade – creating something useful or beautiful out of miscellaneous materials and relishing the process as much as the end product.

SISTERS UNITE

It wasn't until I got a bit older that I started to think about craft in a more serious way. And it was only through my entry into one of the UK's largest women's organizations, the Women's Institute, that I finally began to see its truly empowering potential to build bonds and allow communities to share common threads.

The WI is one of the most misunderstood women's organizations in history and until recently it was suffering from a serious image problem. But, thanks to a fresh and vibrant influx of young blood, I'm happy to say this has started to change.

Originating in Ontario, Canada, in 1897, the organization initially developed as a way to revitalize rural communities and promote opportunities for female education and learning. The first British meeting took place in North Wales in 1915, and the WI soon became closely associated with the women's suffrage movement. Early WI groups offered a peaceful, non-militant way to carry on the 'Votes for Women' campaign during wartime. Many well-known suffragette leaders became active founding members of the various groups that sprang up around the country, including Virginia Woolf, who acted as treasurer to her local WI.

Non-party political and non-religious, the WI and its members did not engage in activities that actively contributed towards the war effort but chose instead to participate in other community services and charitable work. Legendary now for their jam making, they were famously involved with wartime food preservation and production, helping to feed an undernourished nation at the height of rationing. The movement also helped women to set up cooperative markets where they could sell their own handcrafts and home-grown produce to earn money, supplementing their incomes and becoming more self-sufficient. Craftwork has always been at the forefront of WI activities, and the movement aims to revive traditional skills among its members, to raise the profile of craftwork and give it a public status.

SHOREDITCH SISTERS

Yet the WI is so much more than just a collection of crafty ladies, and over the years it has become a cultural force to be reckoned with, often in the vanguard of the cutting edge. In 1943, the WI lobbied for equal opportunities for women ('Equal Pay for Equal Work') and their campaigns have usually been way ahead of the times. The movement helps to mobilize its members to rally together and seek change on issues as wide-ranging and far-reaching as climate change, world poverty and domestic violence. Members are positively encouraged to take an active part in public life. And being part of the WI provides members with a platform to voice their opinions and an opportunity to be heard because, more often than not, when the WI speaks, the nation listens.

The Shoreditch Sisters (as we later came to be known) helped to reintroduce a new generation of young women to what had been one of the most radical and significant grass roots women's movements in the UK to date.

So it was for all these reasons and more that back in 2007 I decided it would be an exciting idea to start up a new group with some friends in Shoreditch, in the heart of London's gritty East End. This may seem an unlikely setting for a group of girls half the age of the average WI member to gather together and meet for underground bake-off competitions and subversive sewing. But so began what was to become a watershed moment for the urban WI movement. The Shoreditch Sisters (as we later came to be known) helped to reintroduce a new generation of young women to what had been one of the most radical and significant grass roots women's movements in the UK to date.

Initially, I thought it would be a fun way to get my girlfriends together once a month – boyfriends would be dismissed for the evening. And being part of the organization would give us a focus and creative outlet for our ideas and love of crafts. So far from trying to shake off the traditional image of the WI, which had a twin set and blue rinse reputation and had been failing to attract a younger membership, the Shoreditch Sisters looked beyond the stereotypes and embraced both craftwork and campaigning. And we seemed to tap into a wider cultural movement that was happening at the time – from the beginning, we stirred the interest of the public and the press alike.

Within our first year, we had been featured in almost every national newspaper. As a result, girls living in far-off towns and cities got in touch asking for advice on how to get involved and new groups were formed all across the country. Our message even travelled across the globe – we made it big in Japan and now have our very own tribute group, the Tokyo Sisters, who, although not officially affiliated with the WI, like to share ideas, projects and causes with us from the opposite side of the world, united in international sisterhood.

So traditions have come full circle, and the Shoreditch Sisters have helped to propel the new WI revolution forward, re-establishing the movement as it changes to meet the needs of modern women. Today, it has hundreds of thousands of members nationwide and is attracting a new generation seeking to reconnect with 'forgotten' skills. The recent urban renewal of the movement has also helped to rebuild social networks and communities as the need to share common bonds and friendship has transcended the divide between town and country.

The WI welcomes all kinds of women from all walks of life, and if you fancy getting in on the action, see p. 233 for my insider tips on starting your own group.

SHOREDITCH SISTERS
homemade
STRAWBERRY
JAM

The Cava Collective Present

Tea Dance & Rock N Roll Night

VIVA CAKE

The Urban Voodoo Machine

4.30 PM TIL 2AM - SATURDAY 20th
FREE TEA, CAKES AND

BECOME YOUR OWN QUEEN OF CRAFTS

Of course, you don't have to join the WI to get involved – all you really need to become your own queen of crafts is the will to express your own individual personality and style. Learning to craft is all about daring to be free and having the confidence to experiment, customize and play around with colour, fabrics, techniques, recipes and stitches.

This book has been inspired in part by the many busy hands and minds that have sparked the fire of my own creative energies, beginning with the moment my great-granny Dolly taught me that first electric stitch. So I hope that you too will be encouraged to kick-start your own creativity and try out some of my easy step-by-step projects, whether you're already a dab hand at crafting or just starting out. Use your imagination to jazz up your world and have a go at stitching a cake-shaped pincushion (see p. 70), make *Alice in Wonderland*-inspired marmalade (p. 143), bake domino petits fours (p. 114) or plant a victory garden (p. 158); the choice is yours!

Or get inspired to reignite some community spirit, as crafting with friends will keep you in stitches both metaphorical and for real. Check out my useful tips on how to set up and run your own sewing circles and old-fashioned quilting bees, as well as host a handful of other fun and friendly get-togethers like crafternoons, fabric exchanges and tea parties (pp. 218–23).

Now, the only thing left to say is that I urge you with all my might to approach the projects on the following pages in the spirit of anarchy. Remember, there are no rules when it comes to crafts. Feel free to weave in and out of the chapters and pick and mix the projects as you are so inspired. If you see something you like, don't be afraid to just give it a go. When we were growing up, my dad always told my sister and me that we could do anything we liked – all we needed was guts and determination. So I want to pass that same message on to you. Don't come apart at the seams if you make a mistake (you always learn from them in the end), but try to love your own small inconsistencies and imperfections – they are what make your creations personal and fiercely one of a kind, just like you. Over time and through practice, skill and technique will always improve, so don't sweat the small stuff when starting out and, above all, have fun.

Now join the revolution and make something!

PART 1

HAND

WOOLCRAFT·STITC

CRAFT

CRAFT·PATCHWORK

Woolcraft

Knitting is the age-old practice of looping and knotting wool together using only your hands and a pair of knitting needles to create fabric. It has been done for centuries and gone through countless cyclical revivals – recently it has reached a fever pitch of popularity and cast off its traditional fusty image for good, becoming a glamorous and even rebellious pastime.

Knit graffiti (aka 'yarn bombing'), using colourful displays of knitting and crochet to tag and beautify outside urban spaces, has helped to change the face of knitting by bringing the craft out of the home and on to the streets. Stitching circles have sprung up all over the world as celebrities, artists and activists alike are learning the knitty-gritty of this exquisitely expressive and exciting craft. (Check pp. 218–19 for ideas on how to start up your own group.) No wonder, as not only is knitting a satisfying pastime but there is nothing more fun than getting together for a good old knit'n'natter to share skills and stitching stories with friends.

The knitting boom has also kick-started a buzz around crafts in general and the yarn revolution has inspired a whole new generation of keen crafters to rediscover centuries-old techniques and reclaim them as relevant and radical. And knitting was one of the first crafts that got me hooked on the handmade, so for that reason it will always hold a special place in my heart. But although my great-grandmother taught me my first stitches while I was still in single digits, I didn't keep it up back then and it wasn't until I hit my late teens that I got the urge to knit again. As neither my mother nor my grandmother had the skills (and great-granny Dolly was sadly no longer around), I had to look elsewhere for my next knitting fix. After asking

around, I found a new teacher – a total gent (yep, a man) who took pity on my meagre student budget and very kindly agreed to teach me for free. So every other Saturday morning, I went to his house for my lesson and his enthusiasm had me reading patterns and stitching up all sorts of complicated shaping techniques after only a handful of sessions.

And that there is one of the best things about knitting – you don't have to be an expert to do it. All you need is a dash of determination and quite literally a handful of equipment: a ball of yarn, a pair of needles, a pattern and that's it, you're good to go. Because you only really need these few things to knit, it's also a thoroughly modern and mobile hobby that fits in perfectly with our hectic lifestyles. I love to keep idle hands busy while travelling on the bus or the train and it's guaranteed to inspire smiles and friendly knitting banter.

When I first started knitting, many of my friends thought I was mad and used to call me 'Granny Jazz' (charming, I know). But they soon learnt the error of their ways, got hip to the stitch and now they beg me to teach them! Once you have learnt to knit, it will be a skill you have for life and you can knit for fun, for yourself, for friends or even for the world (see p. 45).

MAKE DO AND MEND

Yarn Backwards

No one is quite sure exactly where or when knitting evolved – most likely through a basic human need for warmth and protection against the elements – but the earliest knitted artefacts date back all the way to ancient Egypt. Since then, knitting has enjoyed a long and rich history, involving all manner of characters from Queen Elizabeth I (whose obsession with fine knitted stockings prompted a thriving English trade) to the ladies who 'knitted for victory' during the two world wars. A national craze for knitting was ignited during the Second World War and women were at it everywhere, click-clacking away both for the troops and to clothe their families. The Make Do and Mend movement (see p. 196) saw to it that every scrap of yarn was made use of, and old woollies were continually unravelled and reknitted to create brand-new clothes.

But after so long up front, knitting fell out of fashion as factory-made clothes became more available. The popularity of hand knitting really took a nosedive during the 80s and it stopped being widely taught in schools. (I know I was never taught a single stitch, knitting, sewing or otherwise.)

It wasn't until 1999, when American knitter and editor of feminist magazine *Bust*, Debbie Stoller, published her seminal book, *Stitch 'n Bitch*, that knitting resurfaced as a fun and fashionable pastime for the modern girl. And thank god for that, since whatever the motivation for picking up the needles, knitting has always provided a therapeutic distraction.

The relaxing nature of knitting as a meditative craft is definitely something to wax lyrical about. Creating order from chaos, as you fashion something from a disorganized ball of yarn, brings a sense of calm and satisfaction to the maker. I find it so relaxing, in fact, that I can only ever watch a scary movie if I have my knitting to hand. Who knew Hammer Horror and knitting could be compatible? It's recently been suggested that knitting helps improve concentration and brain functionality – it must be all that hand–eye coordination. Of course, besides being good for you, knitting is also a creative act of self-expression that is being enjoyed by the young and old alike. And it looks like this time it's here to stay.

Get Hooked

Once you fall hook, line and sinker for knitting, you will want to start your own collection of tools, but this won't add up to much. All you really need to get going is a pair of needles, a ball of yarn and your hands – it couldn't be simpler.

Knitting Kit and Caboodle

Needles

Knitting needles come in an assortment of different lengths and sizes ranging from super thin to super chunky. The diameter of the needles will affect the size of the stitches; the general rule is the thicker the needle, the looser and more open your stitches will be. Thin needles will create a much tighter and more delicate-looking knitted fabric. Of course, you can play around with needle size to your own advantage and experiment with different yarns to create unique combinations and textures. Try creating a mock-lace effect by knitting very fine yarn with chunky needles, or even try using two different-sized needles for a stretchy effect (see p.33 for a luxurious shimmer scarf project that makes the most of this top-notch technique).

Knitting needle sizes are given in metric, US and old UK sizes, just to make things confusing. So my best advice is to keep a needle gauge and a chart (see p. 25) handy so you can always double-check you have the right needles for the right project. Needles can be made from all kinds of materials, including plastic, metal, bamboo and wood, and which you use is up to you. But I never will understand why modern plastic and metal needles all come in that uninspiring shade of orthopaedic grey. Knitting is a craft from which much of the enjoyment comes from the materials you have in your hands, so why so many modern needles look as if they belong on a hospital ward beats me – I mean, really, would it kill someone to design something with a bit of sparkle?

The most important thing to keep in mind when choosing a pair of needles is that they feel comfortable in your hands and the stitches can be easily knitted from one needle to the other. I love to collect pretty vintage knitting needles, which can be picked up from charity shops for pennies; they usually come in an assortment of bright pastel plastics and allow my stitches to slide on and glide off effortlessly. However, for novice knitters, whose stitches may be more prone to falling off slippery needles, a pair of bamboo pins may be the better buy as the rougher texture will prevent any accidents.

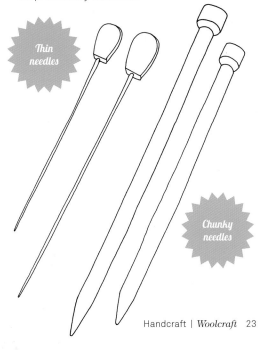

Thin needles

Chunky needles

The most important thing to keep in mind when choosing a pair of needles is that they feel comfortable in your hands and the stitches can be easily knitted from one needle to the other. I love to collect pretty vintage knitting needles, which can be picked up from charity shops for pennies; they usually come in an assortment of bright pastel plastics and allow my stitches to slide on and glide off effortlessly.

1. Yarn

Choosing yarn is a bit like stepping into a sweet shop – there is such an incredible bounty of wool and yarn to choose from in a wild variety of different textures, weights, colours and fibres (both natural and man-made): wool, cotton, silk, nylon, acrylic and combinations of all of them. Each yarn will yield a different result, so when selecting which one to work with you will have to consider what's appropriate to your particular project. Yarns made from luxury natural fibres like mohair, alpaca, angora or cashmere can be expensive but will be well worth it if you want to make something to wear against the skin. Cheaper novelty and acrylic wools are cheerful and fun to use for everything else.

Yarns come in an assortment of different weights and are named accordingly. Familiarize yourself with them before you start a project so you know your double knit from your super chunky.

4-ply A lightweight yarn used for making fine garments like baby clothing and socks.
Double knitting (DK) A light- to mediumweight yarn also often used for baby garments but about twice as thick as 4-ply.
Aran A mediumweight yarn roughly twice the thickness of DK. Great for scarves, hats, sweaters and blankets.
Chunky A chunky yarn perfect for beginners, it's about twice the thickness of Aran. Great for knitting up scarves, gloves and hats.
Super chunky The chunkiest of all yarns is knitted on supersize needles and is loads of fun because it knits up so quick. Too bulky for clothing but fantastic for accessories, cushions and blankets.

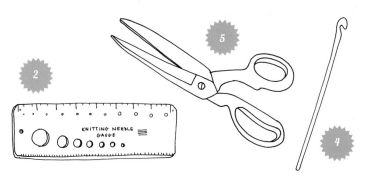

Yarn is typically sold in 50–100 g balls or skeins and always comes with a label that gives all the relevant information regarding weight, dye lot (see below), fibre content and suggested needle size and tension (see p. 23). So it's a wise idea to hold on to the label so that you can refer back to it if need be.

Always remember to buy enough yarn to finish off a project on your first shop, as no two dye-lots will ever be the same. If you do need to go back to the shop to buy more, it may be difficult to find the exact shade to match the yarn you began your project with. I have made this mistake countless times and always kick myself later. So save yourself some self-reproach and sort it out now – it's always better to be safe than sorry.

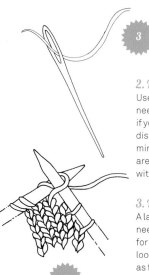

2. Needle Gauge
Useful for checking needle sizes (especially if your knitting bag is a disorganized mess like mine). Vintage needles are often not marked with their size.

3. Darning Needle
A large blunt-pointed needle will be essential for weaving in those loose yarn ends as well as for stitching up your finished knits.

4. Crochet Hook
Smaller than a knitting needle, and with a little hook at one end, a crochet hook is handy for picking up dropped stitches, as well as for making up tassels and finishing (see pp. 46–7 for some knitted bling).

5. Scissors
You will need a small pair of scissors for snipping your yarn ends.

6. Swag Bag
And last but by no means least, don't forget a knitting swag bag to keep all your kit together (see p. 78 to find out how to make your own).

7. Patterns
Before you actually start knitting, you will need to find a pattern that gets your fingers itching to stitch. And you should have no problem in that department; just see pp. 32 onwards to start getting inspired. But if you are completely new to knitting, you might want to start by making a simple square swatch.

Metric	Old UK	US
2 mm	14	0
2.25 mm	13	1
2.75 mm	12	2
3 mm	11	–
3.25 mm	10	3
3.5 mm	–	4
3.75 mm	9	5
4 mm	8	6
4.5 mm	7	7
5 mm	6	8
5.5 mm	5	9
6 mm	4	10
6.5 mm	3	10.5
7 mm	2	–
7.5 mm	1	–
8 mm	0	11
9 mm	0	13
10 mm	0	15
12 mm	–	17
16 mm	–	19
19 mm	–	35
25 mm	–	50

How to Read a Knitting Pattern

If you've never read a knitting pattern before, don't be frightened by abbreviations that at first sight might resemble equations only Einstein himself could decipher. It's just a matter of getting used to the lingo so keep your cool, study the list of abbreviations below (they'll become second nature soon enough, I promise) and make sure you follow the pattern row by row.

—

K knit

P purl

Dec decrease

Inc increase

M1 make 1 stitch

St(s) stitch(es)

Rep repeat

Tog together

K2tog knit 2 together

P2tog purl 2 together

Skp slip one, knit one, pass slipped stitch over

Sl1, k1, psso as above

Cont continue

WS wrong side

RS right side

Col colour

St st stocking stitch

G st garter stitch

* repeat the instructions following an asterisk as indicated in the pattern

Learning the Ropes – How to Knit

Learning to knit really is easy and once you've mastered the basic knit and purl stitches (the only two stitches you will ever need), you will be knitting up a storm in no time.

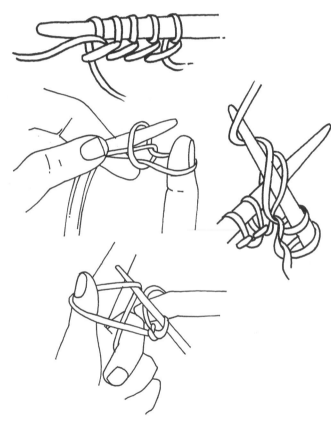

The knit stitch is the most common stitch there is and with this alone you will be able to knit a gorgeous garter-stitch scarf (see p. 32 for a chunky-knit project). I defy absolutely anyone not to be able to master it. The purl stitch is also extremely easy – it's just a backwards knit stitch. Besides these two stitches, all that's left to learn is how to cast on and cast off.

How to Cast On

Before you can begin to knit, you will need to 'cast on' a foundation row of stitches on to one of your needles. There are several different ways to cast on, just as there are several different ways to hold a pair of needles, but I find the easiest is a technique using one needle and your hands (referred to as the 'thumb method'). Here's how you do it:

1. To make the first stitch on the needle, you need to make a slipknot. Take a length of yarn about 25 cm long and cross the working end (the end attached to the ball) over the loose end to form a circle. Hold the loop where the two strands meet and, with your other hand, bring the working end through the middle of the loop from behind to create a new loop. Put this new loop on your needle and pull the two strands of yarn below to tighten. This is your first stitch.

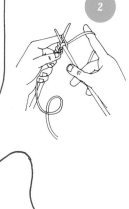

2. To get the next stitch on your needle, hold the needle in one hand and wind the working yarn once around the thumb of your other hand. Hold it taut (and hold the slipknot in place with your forefinger), then insert the tip of the needle under and up through the loop on your thumb. Now let go of the loop and pull the yarn end below, and there you have your second stitch.

3. Continue like this until you have the required number of stitches on your needle. Keep the stitches even and close together to ensure you create a neat edge.

How to Make a Knit Stitch

Now you have your first row of stitches, it's time to knit them! The first row you knit after casting on can be tricky as the stitches will be quite tight against the needle. When making knit stitches, you must always keep the yarn you are knitting with at the back of the work.

1. Hold the needle with the cast-on stitches on in your left hand. Then insert your right-hand needle from front to back into the front of your first cast-on stitch. Holding the working end of the yarn (the end attached to the ball) clasped in your right hand, use your right index finger to wrap the yarn around the tip of the right-hand needle.

2. Then draw this wound yarn down and to the front of the left needle to pull a new loop through the first stitch.

3. Slowly allow the old stitch to drop off the left-hand needle, keeping your newly created stitch on your right-hand needle.

4. Now repeat this action (making sure you keep the yarn at the back of your work) until you have knitted all your cast-on stitches and transferred them from the left-hand needle to the right. And that's your first row!

5. To start knitting the next row, turn the work around so that the right-hand needle is in your left hand with the yarn at the beginning of the row, ready to stitch as before.

How to Make a Purl Stitch

Purling is like knitting backwards. So when working purl stitches you will need to keep the yarn at the front of the work rather than at the back.

How to Cast Off

When your last row has been stitched, you are ready to cast off. This simply means removing your knitting from the needles without unravelling the work.

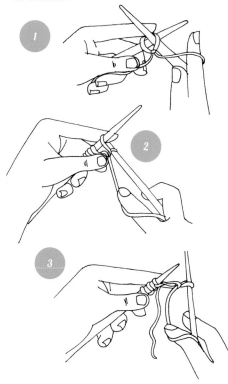

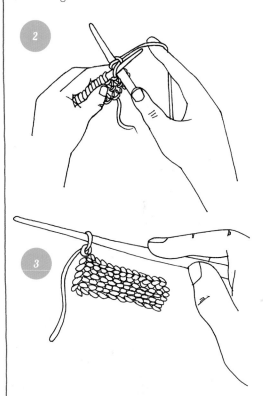

1. Hold the needle with the cast-on stitches on in your left hand. Then insert your right-hand needle from back to front into the front of the first stitch. Wrap the working yarn around the tip of the right-hand needle.

2. Draw this wound yarn down and to the back of the left-hand needle to pull a new loop through the first stitch.

3. Slowly allow the old stitch to drop off the left-hand needle, keeping your newly created stitch on your right-hand needle.

4. Repeat this action (making sure you keep the yarn at the front of your work) until all the stitches have been purled and transferred from your left-hand needle to your right.

1. Knit two stitches as normal (see above).

2. Use the tip of the left-hand needle to pick up the first stitch and bring it up and over the top of the second stitch before allowing it to drop off the needle altogether, leaving you with just one stitch on the right-hand needle. You have just cast off your first stitch!

3. Knit another stitch as normal and repeat step 2. Keep going, knitting a stitch, then removing a stitch, until you are left with one last stitch on the right-hand needle.

4. Snip the working end of the yarn, leaving at least 10 cm, and pull the yarn through the last stitch on the needle to make a knot that sits firmly against the knitting. The tail end can then be woven into your work with a darning needle to secure.

Some Hints and Tips for Newbie Knitters or Those Dusting Off Their Rusty Needles

To practise stitches and casting on, use a pair
of 4 mm knitting needles and a ball
of double knitting yarn.

Never leave knitting in the middle of a row,
as the yarn is likely to pull and create an
uneven tension or – even more disastrous –
fall off the needles altogether!

Always leave your knitting at the end of
a knit row; that way you will always know
what stitch you finished on and where to
pick up again.

Always count your stitches once you have knitted
a new row to check you have the right number
and haven't accidentally made an extra stitch
or dropped a stitch.

When starting a new ball of yarn, always use
the yarn end from the inside of the ball – this will make
it easier to unravel as you knit. To find the yarn end and
avoid yarn vomit (when the tangled wool inside the ball
spills out), wiggle your finger into the centre of the ball
to locate the loose end and then pull it out gently.

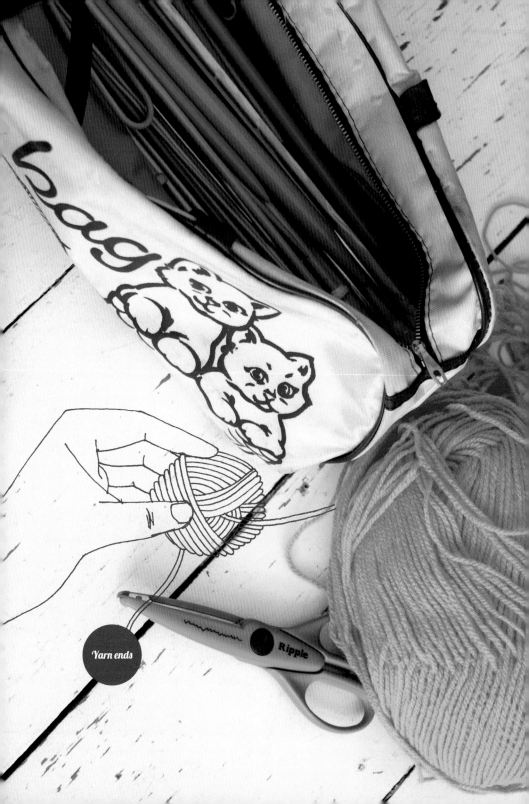

Yarn ends

Ripple

Scarf Out – Knitting Scarves

Now you know the basics, it's time to put your new skills to the test. Start with a scarf, which is just a matter of casting on, knitting away until you have a nice long piece of fabric and then casting off. Simple!

It's the best way to practise and build your confidence before you move on to the more complicated stuff, and when I first started out, I made one for just about anyone who would let me. I even started teaching my friends. As a birthday present for one particular girlfriend, I bought a big bundle of red and purple yarn with the intention of helping her to knit a stripy scarf any Bay City Roller groupie would be proud of. We definitely had fun knitting together, but I have to admit her scarf ended up looking like a creature from a science fiction movie as she dropped and picked up stitches at an alarming rate and refused my offer of help. I salute her determination but let it be a warning: keep an eye on your stitches and count them after every row, just to make doubly sure you've got the right number on your needles.

Fast-Knitting Chunky Scarf

Chunky yarn is my favourite as it knits up so quickly – instant-gratification knitting. Visit your local yarn shop and invest in some colourful chunky yarn and a pair of chunky needles, then get busy knitting up a scarf in plain and simple garter stitch. Follow the pattern below for a cosy scarf to wear on wintry evenings, then jazz up both ends with garlands of tassels or plenty of pompoms (see pp. 46–9). This pattern is so easy, yet oh so effective.

You will need:
- Needles: 7 – 10 mm
- Yarn: 6 x 50 g balls bulky yarn (Rowan Big Wool would be ideal)

Making:
Cast on 30 sts
Knit in garter stitch (see p. 38) until the scarf measures 195 cm from the cast-on edge (for an extra-neat edge, slip the first stitch of every row)
Cast off all sts

Pussy-Bow Scarf

Self-striping yarn is the way to go for this super-cute pussy-bow scarf (to be worn around the neck doubled up into a bow-tie). It's the hassle-free way to create stripes and is available in a variety of colour combinations. Use a small to medium-sized needle (3 or 3.5 mm will do the trick), then pick out your self-striping sock yarn of choice. I used black and grey, which will look darling when paired with a preppy white shirt and should make your winter woollies transition sweetly from autumn to spring. Knit this up in garter stitch as I have done, or try moss stitch (see p. 38) or even stocking stitch (this will curl at the edges) – the choice is yours.

You will need:
- Needles: 3.5 mm
- Yarn: 1 x 100 g ball of DK self-striping yarn

Making:
Cast on 12 sts
Knit in garter stitch (see p.38) until the scarf measures 185 cm from the cast-on edge (for an extra-neat edge, slip the first stitch of every row)
Cast off all sts

Fast-Knitting Chunky Scarf

Pussy-Bow Scarf

Striped Skinny Shimmer Scarf

Striped Skinny Shimmer Scarf

The next step in your scarf-knitting career is to introduce a second colour and get stripy, which only requires you to know how to bring a new ball of yarn into play (see box, right). This super-slinky stylish scarf is knitted with two different-sized needles, to create a slightly stretchy effect which becomes luxurious with the addition of mohair, alpaca or a dash of shimmer yarn.

You will need:
- Needles: 1 x 4 mm and 1 x 9 mm
- Yarn: 2 x 50 g balls of Rowan Alpaca Cotton in contrasting colours and 1 x 50 g ball of Rowan Shimmer

Making:
Cast on 16 sts using the first colour of the Alpaca Cotton and the 4 mm needle
Rows 1 – 6: Knit in garter stitch (see p. 38)
Join the shimmer yarn
Rows 7–8: Knit in garter stitch using both yarns
Drop the shimmer yarn
Rows 9–14: Knit in garter stitch using Alpaca Cotton only
Switch to second colour of Alpaca Cotton
Rows 15–20: Knit in garter stitch
Join the shimmer yarn
Rows 21–2: Knit in garter stitch using both yarns
Drop the shimmer yarn
Rows 23–8: Knit in garter stitch using Alpaca Cotton only
Repeat rows 1–28 until scarf measures 260 cm from the cast-on edge
Cast off all sts

Joining Yarn

As your knitting grows, at some point you will come to the end of your first ball of yarn and you will need to join another ball to carry on. Or you may want to join a new colour to create a stripy effect (as in the shimmer scarf project below). Always try to do this at the end of a row, as this will make a cleaner join. Simply leave the old yarn hanging, and knit the next row with your new yarn. The first few stitches will feel slightly unstable so be sure to knit them carefully. Then just knot the two tail ends of yarn together to secure (you can hide them later by weaving them back into your work with a darning needle).

Shaping

Straight knitting (or purling) in rows will yield a long piece of rectangular fabric. If you want to knit any other shape, you will have to add or remove stitches.

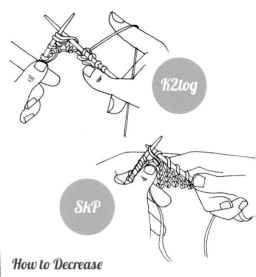

In knitting terms, this is known as increasing and decreasing and is how knitted garments are 'shaped' by being made either wider or narrower at certain points.

How to Increase

Increasing stitches makes the knitted fabric wider, by adding new stitches. The two most common ways to do this are:

— The Increase stitch (inc): knit a stitch as normal but instead of letting the old stitch drop off, leave it on the left-hand needle. Then knit into the back of that same stitch to create an extra stitch. Here you have made two stitches out of one.

— The Make One stitch (m1): insert the tip of your left-hand needle under the horizontal strand of yarn that lies between two stitches, then either knit or purl into the front or the back of the picked-up strand (as directed). Here you have created a new stitch between two existing stitches.

How to Decrease

Decreasing removes stitches from the needles to make your knitting narrower. Here are a couple of ways you can do this:

— Knit two stitches together (k2tog): insert the right-hand needle into the front of the next two stitches and knit them together as one – or purl them together (p2tog) if you are on a purl row. This method is usually used at the beginning of a row.

— Slip one, knit one, pass slipped stitch over (Skp or Sl1, k1, psso): slip the next stitch from the left-hand needle to the right without knitting or purling it, then knit or purl the next stitch as normal. Then, using the tip of your left-hand needle, pick up the slipped stitch and pass it up and over the top of the knit stitch and then off the right-hand needle altogether. This method is usually used at the end of a row.

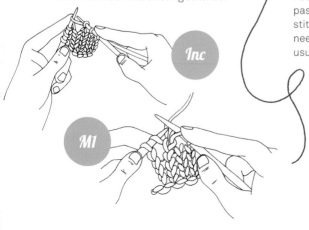

Dropped Stitches

Dropped stitches are an inevitable part of learning to knit. But don't worry, as you get more practised you'll find they happen with less frequency until one day you realize you haven't dropped a stitch in ages. The sooner you notice a dropped stitch, the easier it is to fix. If you don't address the problem right away, your knitting will begin to unravel and a ladder of holes will form within the work. If the stitch has dropped only one row below, it's easy to fix. Just use the tip of your knitting needle to pick it up and place it back on to the other needle, catching and pulling the loose strand above through the loop as you go. If the stitch has dropped several rows below, you'll need to use a crochet hook to pick the stitch up, either through the front for a knit stitch, or from behind for a purl stitch. Insert the hook through the loop of the dropped stitch, then pull the stitch up to catch the horizontal yarn thread immediately above and pull it through. Keep hooking the loop stitch back up until you reach the row you were knitting, then slip the stitch back on to the needle and continue to knit or purl as normal.

Don't worry, we've all been there! If you're completely new to knitting, sometimes the best way to master it is a one-to-one lesson. Visit a local knitting group or find a friend or relative to help you out. It should only take one session before you get the hang of things, then all you gotta do is practise, practise, practise. Wool gatherings are helpful for knitters of all skill levels, as you get to share knitting know-how among like-minded friends. (Whenever I head to a new town, I always like to find out where the nearest club meets.) Or if you're stuck at home and feeling like you're at the end of your rope with this knitting lark, check out YouTube, which has some brilliant how-to videos and demonstrations.

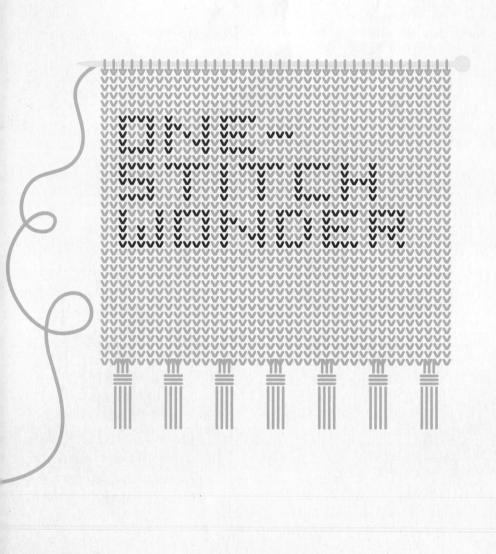

Stick That on Your Needles and Knit It!
– Experimenting with Stitch Patterns

'Stitch pattern' simply means a particular combination of individual stitches (usually knits and purls) that creates a certain texture to your knitting – and they can turn a boring piece of knitting into a fancy thing.

Use the right combination of knits, purls and a few little tricks and you can create a stretchy rib, delicate lace, chunky cable, bobbles and brocades or even a cute little bumpy heart. There are just three things to keep in mind before you start experimenting:

Some stitch patterns must be worked in multiples or include extra numbers of stitches, so it's best to double check before starting out that the stitch pattern will be compatible with your project.

Take care when alternating between purl and knit stitches to make sure that the yarn is on the correct side of the work for the stitch being knitted (at the back of the work when you're knitting and at the front of the work when purling).

It's always a good idea to knit up some swatches before you jump into a project that calls for a stitch pattern you haven't tried before – that way you can practise your stitches and iron out any little inconsistencies before you begin.

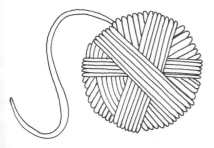

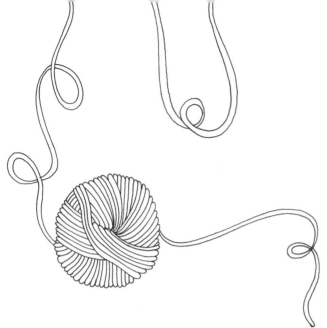

So don't be a one-stitch wonder! Here are some basic stitch patterns to try out to create both plain and textured knitting. Just work the row combinations in each pattern over and over until you have a nice long piece of fabric.

Garter Stitch (g st)
The most basic stitch pattern, garter stitch is made up from continuous rows of knitting (i.e., no purling in sight). It creates a reversible, solid, flat fabric with the bumps of the stitches set out in neat horizontal rows.

Knit every row

Garter Ridge
A pretty alternative to garter stitch that throws a purl row into the mix.

Row 1 : K
Row 2 : P
Row 3 : K
Row 4 : K

Stocking Stitch (st st)
One of the most common knitting stitch patterns, stocking stitch is formed by working a row of knit stitches (always begin with a knit row!) and alternating with a purl row. The front is neat and smooth with all the stitches in tidy little rows of interlocking V-shapes, while the back is ridged with knobbly-looking bumpy stitches. The edges of stocking-stitch fabric have a tendency to curl in, so if you are using it to knit a flat item that will not be joined or seamed then you will have to create borders (a few garter stitches added at the edges will prevent curling).

Row 1 : K
Row 2 : P

Single Rib (k1, p1)
This creates a stretchy reversible fabric used where a close fit is needed, like cuffs, collars, necks and waistbands. It is created by knitting a stitch, then purling a stitch, all the way along the row.

The number of cast-on stitches must be a multiple of 4
All rows : K1, p1; rep to end of row

Double Rib (k2, p2)
The number of cast-on stitches must be a multiple of 4
All rows : K2, p2; rep to end of row

Moss Stitch
Moss stitch (known as seed stitch in the US) is one of my all-time favourite stitches to knit, as I love swinging between the knit and purl stitches. It's a cute little pattern that gets its name from the raised dimple effect of the stitches, which resembles moss or little seeds. It creates a firmer fabric than garter or stocking stitch.

The number of cast-on stitches must be a multiple of 2
Row 1 : K1, p1; rep to end of row
Row 2 : P1, k1; rep to end of row

Double Moss Stitch
The number of cast-on stitches must be a multiple of 4
Row 1 : K2, p2; rep to end of row
Row 2 : Rep row 1
Row 3 : P2, k2; Rep to end of row
Row 4 : Rep row 3

Garter Stitch

Double Moss Stitch

Stocking Stitch

Moss Stitch

Single Rib

Double Rib

Off the Hook – Knitted Headbands

These off-the-hook knitted headbands will keep your head warm and stylish. They are ridiculously easy to knit and are the perfect portable project – so small they can be carried in your handbag and broken out for a spot of lunch-break knitting. Cosy and cool, a headband can really make or break your outfit, but best of all – no hat hair!

Oh So Clara Bow Knitted Turban Headband

Turbans conjure up flapper girls, silent movie stars and all things vintage glam. (Clara Bow is one of my style icons of all time!) So what makes more sense than a knitted turban? Update your look by wearing on its own or stick a big jewelled or beaded brooch in the middle of the gather for an exotic touch.

You will need:

- Needles: 5 mm
- Yarn: 1 x 50 g ball of DK yarn in black
- Darning needle

Making:

For the headband:
Cast on 26 sts
Row 1: K6, p4, k6, p4, k6
Row 2: P6, k4, p6, k4, p6
Repeat rows 1–2 for 105 rows
Cast off all sts

Joining Seams

When joining two knitted seams together, use a darning needle and matching yarn. Before sewing up, lay your knits out flat on a table, matching seam edges side by side, and pin together at wide intervals. For most knits, you can either simply oversew the edges to join or use a backstitch. To oversew a seam, match the knitting up with right sides of the knitted fabric facing together, then make a series of slanted stitches against the seam edge. For backstitch, always sew the seam from the wrong side of the fabric. Begin by aligning the two pieces with right sides facing together, then start to backstitch (see p. 61). Try to keep this stitch as close to the seam edge as possible to prevent any extra bulkiness being created in the seam allowance.

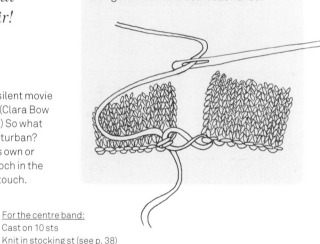

For the centre band:
Cast on 10 sts
Knit in stocking st (see p. 38)
for 20 rows
Cast off all sts

To make up:
Sew the two ends of the headband strip together to make a band. Place the small centre strip around the seam of the headband and sew the two ends together on the inside, working a couple of fix stitches (see p. 62) to hold the two pieces together.

Girlie Bow Headband

This delightfully darling bow-fronted headband is an absolute must for your winter wardrobe. Knit up in a rich scarlet red, it will look positively dramatic and suit brunettes and blondes alike. And if you're feeling playful, swap the bow for a pompom (see p. 48).

You will need:
- Needles: 5 mm
- Yarn: 1 x 50 g ball of DK yarn in scarlet red
- Darning needle

Making:
For the headband:
Cast on 25 sts
Knit in stocking st
(see p. 38) for 105 rows
Cast off all sts

For the bow:
Cast on 25 sts
Knit in stocking st for 54 rows
Cast off all sts

For the centre band:
Cast on 12 sts
Knit in stocking st for 20 rows
Cast off all sts

To make up:
Sew the two ends of the headband strip together to make a band. Sew the two ends of the bow strip together to make a band, fold in half and place on top of the headband seam. Place the small centre-band strip around the centre of the bow and sew the two ends together on the inside, working a couple of fix stitches (p. 62) to hold the three pieces together.

Oh So Clara Bow Headband

Girlie Bow Headband

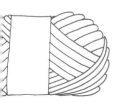

Knitted Snood

A snood should be the next step in your knitting repertoire. This simple version knits up in one rectangular piece; attaching a snap fastening (see p. 74 for how to sew) allows you to curl it round your head and cuddle up.

You will need:

• Needles: 12 mm
• Yarn: 3 x 50 g balls of DK yarn in different shades of grey, 1 x 50 g ball of DK yarn in black, 1 x 50 g ball of DK yarn in light grey
• Pair of snap fasteners

Making:

The three balls of grey yarn and one ball of black are used together as one to create a multi-coloured effect called marling. It's much easier to work if you make one ball of multi-coloured yarn from the individual balls before you begin knitting. The light-grey yarn is used on its own, but use five strands at once to make it nice and thick.

Cast on 71 sts
Rows 1–5: Knit in single rib (see p. 38) using five strands of the light-grey yarn
Switch to multi-coloured yarn (see above)
Row 6: K2tog, k67, k2tog (you should end up with 69 sts on your needle)
Row 7: P
Row 8: K
Row 9: P
Row 10: k2tog, k65, k2tog (you should end up with 67 sts on your needle)
Row 11: P
Row 12: K
Row 13: P
Row 14: K
Row 15: P2tog, p63, p2tog (you should end up with 65 sts on your needle)
Row 16: K
Row 17: P
Row 18: K
Row 19: P
Row 20: K2tog, k61, k2tog (you should end up with 63 sts on your needle)
Row 21: P
Row 22: K
Row 23: P
Row 24: K
Row 25: P2tog, p59, p2tog (you should end up with 61 sts on your needle)
Row 26: K
Row 27: P
Row 28: K
Row 29: P
Row 30: K2tog, k57, k2tog (you should end up with 59 sts on your needle)
Row 31: P
Row 32: K
Row 33: P
Row 34: K
Row 35: P2tog, p55, p2tog (you should end up with 57 sts on your needle)
Row 36: K
Row 37: P
Row 38: K
Row 39: P
Row 40: K2tog, k53, k2tog (you should end up with 55 sts on your needle)
Row 41: P
Row 42: K
Row 43: P
Row 44: K
Row 45: P2tog, p51, p2tog (you should end up with 53 sts on your needle)
Row 46: K
Switch to light-grey yarn
Rows 47–51: Knit in single rib
Cast off all sts

To make up:

Place the snood on your head and pin where you want the snap fastener to be. Sew the snap on the inside of the snood (see p. 74).

Granny Takes a Trip – Knitted Blanket

'Granny squares' are knitted or crocheted squares of fabric that are joined together to make big blankets. Although they are traditionally associated with the retired, knitting squares is the ideal group activity for a knitting circle as you can work the squares individually, then join them up at a later date to create a large afghan blanket, a bedspread or a cushion.

It's also a great way to practise your stitches and a good opportunity to try out some of the pretty stitch patterns on pp. 38–9.

This blindingly bright and psychedelic blanket, made up of individually knitted 15 x 15cm squares, is a tribute to granny-square knitters everywhere. Knit up 36 squares in simple garter stitch – or you could try something fancier (see p. 38). If you do decide to knit up some patterned squares, make sure all your squares are made up from the same number of stitches and create a similar tension.

You will need:

- Needles: 4 mm
- Yarn: any DK yarn in an array of colours

Making:

To make one square:
Cast on 34 sts
Knit in garter stitch (see p. 38) for 52 rows
Cast off all sts

To make up:
Join your 36 squares together in strips of 6 using an overcast stitch (see p. 62). Then join your 6 strips of squares together, with the same stitch. Finish with a blanket stitch (see p. 62) around the edges.

Knit Your Bit

Knitting for charity is an old tradition and a perfect way to channel creative energies into worthwhile causes – you can lend a hand in the community by putting your craft skills to the test and help those in need. Famous volunteer-driven nationwide knitting campaigns of the past, like the Red Cross's wartime 'Knit Your Bit' and 'Our Boys Need Sox' drives, had WI ladies of yesteryear busy knitting with patriotic fervour, stitching up socks, gloves, jumpers, hats and helmet liners for the soldiers serving overseas. And today, charity knitting is still very much alive and kicking as more recent drives continue to receive overwhelming support. Global campaigns like Afghans for Afghans (which sent hand-knitted blankets and clothes to bring comfort and warmth to the people of Afghanistan) or Teddies for Tragedies (which provided hand-knitted toys for children in need) are great examples of how crafting for the greater good has become popular with us modern knitters. My own great-great-grandmother knitted right into her nineties and, half-blind, she continued to stitch scarves and blankets for the homeless and those in need. Charity knitting is a wonderful way to use your creative talents and give back to your community where every stitch counts.

Finishing Touches – Knitted Bling!

A few clever finishing touches will give your hand knits the edge and make them stand out from the crowd. Here are a handful of pretty embellishments and decorations to keep your fingers busy and your knits looking pretty – great for using up those leftover bits of yarn.

Tassels

Tassels are easy to make and can brighten up even the blandest knits. Add tassels to the ends of blankets, the corners of cushion covers or the top of a hat. (Check p. 207 for more DIY fashion ideas and tips to inspire you to tassel up.)

To make your own homemade tassels, you will need some yarn and a cardboard template the size of a standard postcard (10 x 15 cm), or any size you choose – just keep in mind that the length of the card will determine the length of the finished tassel. Then:

1. Wind some yarn around the card (for a long tassel, wind around the length of the card, and for a shorter version, wind around the width) anywhere from 10 to 40 times, depending on the thickness of yarn you are using and how plump you want your tassel to be. Snip the yarn so that it's level with the bottom of the card.

2. Cut another piece of yarn and pass it through all the loops of yarn at the top of the card. Tie securely with a double knot.

3. Remove the card and, holding the tassel at the top, cut the loops of yarn at the bottom.

4. Cut another piece of yarn and tie it about a quarter of the way down from the top of the tassel to create a 'neck'. Wrap the yarn around this point several times and secure with a double knot.

5. Cut the yarn off, leaving a 30 cm strand, and use a darning needle to thread it from the front to the back of the tassel several times to secure. Trim to neaten.

Tassels

Tassel Fringe

A tassel fringe works wonders as a decorative edge for a scarf or blanket (use for the chunky-knit scarf on p. 32), giving a fabulous finish and an extra splash of colour and texture. Use a similar technique as for one tassel, winding your chosen yarn around a postcard or cardboard template. Then:

1. Cut the wound yarn at the bottom edge and remove the template. You will use these short strands of yarn to make your tassel fringe.

2. Thread a darning needle with two or three strands doubled over (all the cut ends going into the eye), then insert the tip of the needle into the edge of the knitted fabric from back to front to create a loop of your stranded yarn.

3. Now pull the needle down through the loop you just created to make a knot that sits tightly against the edge of the knitting, then remove the needle.

4. Do this all the way along the edge of your scarf or blanket, spacing the fringe at even intervals. Trim the ends to create a neat finish.

Knitted Bows

Knitted bows make perfect trimmings not only for your knits but for all your other handcrafted bits and bobs. I like to make customized bows for all sorts of crafty projects, and especially for creating my own accessories or embellishments (check the DIY fashion tips on p. 207). Attach them to metal clasps to wear in your hair, or on to safety pins to fix on to bags, shoes or the front of an old jumper. They also make darling gift trimmings to dress up your parcels (check p. 231 for DIY gift-wrapping ideas).

To make the bows, use any kind of light- to mediumweight yarn and needles to match.

Small Bow

1. Cast on 15 stitches and knit in garter stitch (see p. 38) for 15 cm, then cast off.

2. To make the middle strip, cast on 5 stitches and knit for 8 cm, then cast off.

3. To make up, pinch the middle of the larger knitted rectangle to create a gathered fold, then wrap the small strip of knitting around the centre and secure with a few fix stitches (p. 62).

Large Bow

1. Cast on 30 stitches and knit in garter stitch for 20 cm, then cast off.

2. To make the middle strip, cast on 10 stitches and knit for 10 cm, then cast off.

3. Make up as directed for the small bow (step 3) above.

Bows

How to Make the Perfect Pompom

Pompoms were a girlhood obsession of mine, and to this day I still can't get enough of them. One year, for Christmas, my parents gave me a majorette outfit (for those of you not in the know, majorettes are marching band back-up dancers – yep, totally rock'n'roll). I loved it and used to prance about the house twirling my batons bedecked with flowing streamers, oodles of pompoms and sparkly silver tassels. Pompoms remind me of girlie sleepovers, watching classic 80s flicks like *Pretty in Pink*, and my childhood longing to be a cheerleader. You've gotta love 'em. These playful, fluffy tufts of yarn are guaranteed to snazz up any outfit or accessory. They can be attached as kitsch embellishments to blankets, scarves, bags, hats, mittens, gloves and anything else that tickles your fancy.

You will need:
• Cardboard
• Scissors
• Yarn

Making:

1. Cut out two identical-sized doughnut shapes from some thick cardboard. The diameter of the outer circle will be slightly larger than the diameter of the finished pompom. Cut the inner circle half the size of the outer edge.

2. Wrap the yarn around the two circles, pulling it through the centre hole as you make each pass until the hole gets very small. The more yarn you wind around the cardboard circles, the fuller and fatter your pompom will be.

3. Snip the yarn all around the circumference between the two doughnuts, making sure you cut through all the layers.

4. Cut a long length of yarn and tie tightly between the two doughnuts, securing with a tight knot.

5. Then carefully cut away and ease off the two cardboard doughnuts and shake out your full and fluffy pompom.

6. Finally, trim the yarn here and there to create an evenly shaped pompom, leaving the two long ends for attaching.

The Perfect Pompom

Easy-Peasy Pompoms

There are a number of very nifty plastic pompom makers available to buy from most good craft and haberdashery stores. And lucky for us, ready-made pompom makers come in a variety of sizes ranging from micro mini to jumbo, which means there should always be one to match your requirements.

Pompom Headdresses

My pompom mania knows no bounds but I particularly love to wear them in my hair. Try a jumbo-sized pompom stuck on to an Alice band, either on top or to the side. Or why not try two medium-sized black pompoms perched like Minnie Mouse ears to either side of the head? Three corresponding coloured pompoms worn to the side look demure, as does a garland of pompoms made up in a rainbow of colours.

Pompom Headdress

Pompom Wreath

You will need:

- Hairband – either an Alice band or a ballet band; experiment and see which works best for you
- Glue gun or some strong fabric glue
- Plenty of pompoms!
- Yarn for binding

Making:

1. You might want to cover your headband with yarn first. If you do, draw a line of glue along the top of the headband from one end to the other. Being careful not to get the glue on your hands, wrap yarn around the band until you get to the other end and then secure with a knot or an extra dab of glue. Set aside to dry.

2. Wind your chosen pompoms into place on top of the band using the long tail ends and secure with tight knots. Use a selection of different colours and sizes of pompom for a more avant-garde effect, or keep it classic and work the band with simple shades in a uniform size. Finally, trim off any loose ends and use an extra dab of fabric glue to secure any unravelling threads.

Pompom Wreath

Knock up this oh-so-easy pompom wreath for some festive good cheer to make your front door proud. The perfect excuse to bust out the cheap acrylic sparkly glitter yarn – bad taste rules for handmade holiday fun!

When choosing the colours for your pompoms, don't go overboard – try to stick to just three or four to avoid making the design too busy. You may also want to keep to the classic theme of your chosen holiday – for Christmas, use green, red and white; for Easter, orange, yellow and white; and for Valentine's Day, try pink, red and white sparkles.

You will need:

- Styrofoam wreath base (pick one up from a craft shop – make sure it has a good depth, as you want the pompoms to bunch around, creating a 3D effect)
- Oodles of yarn in festive colours
- Pompom makers, or some cardboard to make your own
- Scissors
- Glue (optional)

Making:

1. Choose a base-colour yarn and wind it around the wreath until it is completely covered. Secure with a knot to the back.

2. Make lots of pompoms in different sizes and colours to give a sense of scale and variety. You may need up to 40 or 50 pompoms, which sounds a hell of a lot, but it's worth the effort to make a lovely plump and fluffy wreath.

3. Attach the pompoms to the front of the wreath, knotting into place at the back until the surface is completely covered. If possible, try to use the same colour yarn to tie the pompoms as you used to wind round the base in step 1 so that the ties won't be visible. And make sure you keep the knots fairly loose, so that you can shuffle the pompoms into position to create the finished look. You don't want them to be squashed together, but you also don't want to see any gaps.

4. When you have finished arranging all your pretty pompoms, attach a string of yarn with some drawing pins to the back and hang up the wreath in prime position. And watch to make sure the neighbours don't nick it!

It's a yarn revolution

start your
sewing stash -
fabrics &
trimmings

a stitch in time
sew out of control

HEY HO!
LET'S SEW

STITCHCRAFT

NOW, I'LL JUST BE UP FRONT AND ACKNOWLEDGE THAT SEWING IS A VAST SUBJECT. SO VAST, IN FACT, THAT I COULD EASILY WRITE A WHOLE BOOK ABOUT IT. BUT DON'T LET THAT PUT YOU OFF — YOU NEED MASTER ONLY A FEW BASIC SKILLS AND YOU'LL BE ARMED FOR LIFE. WITH A SMALL AMOUNT OF EFFORT AND VERY LITTLE EXPENSE, YOU CAN CREATE THE MOST AMAZINGLY SIMPLE YET STUNNING EFFECTS, WHETHER YOU'RE SEWING BY HAND OR ON THE MACHINE (BOTH OF WHICH WE WILL TACKLE IN THIS CHAPTER).

A Stitch in Time Sewing is one of the oldest textile arts – it's been around so long, in fact, that even the ever-resourceful cavemen were hip to the stitch, sewing animal hides with bone needles and thread made from animal sinews and plant fibres. For thousands of years, sewing was done exclusively by hand and, more often than not, by women. (Some ancient shards of pottery show women weaving on looms and even using their needles and spindles as weapons.) For many centuries, domestic sewing was an everyday necessity – women stitched and mended clothes, linens and just about everything else. And this was how it was until the industrial revolution brought a thriving mechanized textile industry and changed the very fabric of women's domestic lives for ever. In the new factories, women's stitching skills were exploited in poor conditions with pay to match. However, there was an upside – domestic sewing machines came not far behind the industrial ones and relieved many women from the tedium of endless hand sewing (although hand sewing remained a necessity for most, especially during the two World Wars when the Make Do and Mend movement was in full swing).

After the Second World War, the women's movement upped the ante and when Betty Friedan exploded on to the scene in 1963 with her seminal feminist text *The Feminine Mystique*, it seemed that domestic sewing's days were numbered. Women everywhere were rethinking their roles and making the move out of the house and into the workplace. Over time, what was traditionally thought of as woman's work came to be shunned and so-called 'feminine' pastimes were trivialized. A sad state of affairs to say the least, and sewing, along with knitting and other crafts, was considered deeply unfashionable for years. Thankfully this is no longer the case and a new generation of stitchers is eager to reclaim that rich heritage of female creative accomplishment.

Learning to sew not only connects you to this long tradition but is also one of the most satisfying and creatively rewarding crafts going. Which is why everyone seems to be at it these days – sewing classes are packed with punters and crafting cafés (where you can get the use of a sewing machine along with your coffee) are cropping up to cater for the itch to stitch.

Sew Out of Control   If you're new to sewing, it may seem a daunting prospect, and I know this because I've been there – it's a bit like being the new girl at school and everybody seems to know more than you. But don't worry, because an exclusive members' club it ain't. In fact, you really don't need any expertise or previous experience to join in, just a willingness to experiment.

I learnt to sew slowly, on my own, and by breaking all the rules, pretty much making up stitches as I went along. But I've also picked up tips and techniques from friends and family (my mother's friend taught me how to sew French seams), so never pass up the opportunity to gain invaluable hand-me-down advice!

Start with a simple project first and don't dive in at the deep end of the sewing basket. Try hand sewing a doughnut-shaped pincushion (see p. 71) or make a sweetly scented lavender bag (p. 167). Completing these will give you the motivation to move on to the next level. Remember – it doesn't have to be perfect for you to have learnt something. And at least you will be able to sing it like Sid Vicious: 'I did it my way!'

START YOUR SEWING STASH

Starting a sewing stash is the first thing a girl's gotta do as soon as she's caught the crafting bug. Now, there's a mind-boggling range of sewing tools on the market to keep you in good stitches but you certainly don't need to rush out and buy them all right away. A good kit should be acquired over time as your skills (and addiction) progress. Similarly with fabrics and trimmings – try to buy these as you need them, to prevent your stash reaching epic proportions.

Fabrics and Trimmings   These days there is a massive and enticing choice of different materials available and one trip to your local haberdashery will send your head spinning. Different fabrics have their own unique qualities and a corresponding list of pros and cons. So while you should feel completely free to mix things up as much as you like and use whatever fabric takes your fancy, it's worth taking the time to get familiar with the options before you splurge. Fabrics can be made with natural fibres like cotton, synthetic fibres like polyester or a combination of both. Cottons are washable, easy to handle and won't stretch. Synthetics are crease-resistant, easy to iron and non-shrinking. For beginners, it's usually best to go for cotton or a combination fabric.

Felt   Unlike most fabrics, felt isn't woven; rather the fibres are chemically bonded together to create a dense, soft, pliable and non-fraying fabric. It is almost always synthetic and comes in a variety of thicknesses. The heavier stuff is the best, as thin felt has a nasty tendency to tear when strained.

Stuffing   Used for filling things like cushions and toys, stuffing looks a bit like wiry cotton wool and is usually sold by the bag. There are different types, but the cheaper polyester is fine: washable and widely available. (You could always use the stuffing from a cheap and cheerful cushion if you find yourself caught out by a filling emergency.)

Wadding　If you want to pad or line anything flat, like a quilt or the laptop case on p. 77, you'll need wadding. Polyester wadding is cheap, washable, readily available and perfect for the smaller projects in this book. For a quilt, cotton wadding is a better option as it is more breathable. Wadding comes in a variety of thicknesses, but be warned: if the wadding is too thick, you won't be able to run it through your sewing machine.

Trimmings　Sequins, beads, buttons and all sorts of other fripperies are useful for embellishing your sewing projects. I tend to buy trimmings as and when they inspire me – not very economical, as I have box upon box of beads, sequins and assorted bits and bobs that hardly ever see the light of day. Try to buy them only when you need them (but don't be afraid to break the rules if you happen upon a perfectly pleasing piece of ribbon or a beautiful button).

SHOPPING

Haberdasheries and craft shops aren't the only places you can pick up fabrics and trimmings, so think outside the box when you're looking for new materials to inspire you. Car boot sales, vintage shops, charity shops and jumble sales can all be fabric treasure troves and you'll often find things that aren't on the rolls in your local haberdashery. Some wholesale shops will sell direct to casual customers – there might be a minimum spend but it shouldn't be very high and, of course, buying in bulk can be more economical. See 'Address Book' on p. 234 for some of my favourite stash haunts.

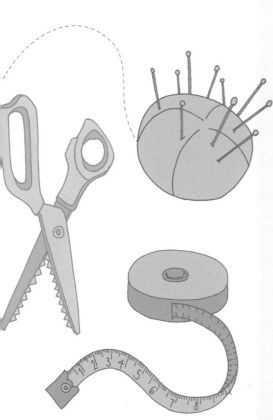

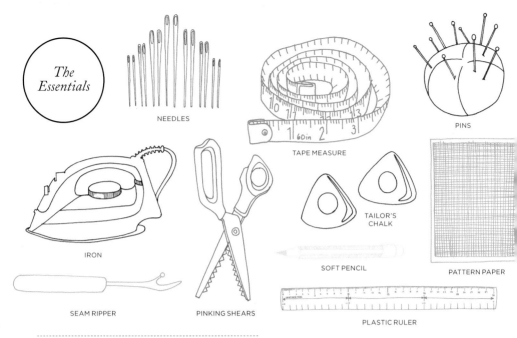

NEEDLES

TAPE MEASURE

PINS

IRON

TAILOR'S CHALK

SOFT PENCIL

PATTERN PAPER

SEAM RIPPER

PINKING SHEARS

PLASTIC RULER

Sewing Box Essentials   Besides fabrics, there are a few other things you will need to get going. As well as the equipment listed below, I also like to keep with me a small portable sewing kit that includes just the bare essentials (threads, pins, needles, scissors, seam ripper) – super useful if you need to sew on the go. Just make sure it's small enough to fit in your handbag.

Needles   Hand-sewing needles come in a range of sizes so invest in a packet of assorted needles to make sure you always have the right kind to hand. Buy the best you can afford too – cheap needles will blunt and bend easily. I also like to have a few self-threading needles (although they're intended for the elderly or visually impaired), which are super nifty with slotted tops (instead of eyes) for easy pop-on and pop-off threading action.

Pins   Pins also come in a variety of lengths and sizes. Generally, small fine dressmaking pins are best; however, for larger work (like the Thunderbird quilt on p. 98), longer pearl or glass-headed pins will be better. Avoid cheap pins that will blunt immediately and never ever use rusted ones (no matter how desperate you are) – they will snag and stain your fabulous

fabrics quicker than a kitty on a corner of the sofa. To keep your pins sitting pretty, you will need somewhere to put them: see pp. 70 – 71 for pincushion projects.

Threads   For most home sewing, good-quality all-purpose cotton or polyester thread will do. Keep a selection of various colours in your sewing box so you'll always be able to match your fabrics. Buying bargain threads is a false economy – they will easily snap and break. It's a bit like building a house with bad foundations. My go-to brands are Coats and Gutermanns.

Scissors   A good pair of fabric scissors will be your best investment. Buy the absolute best pair you can afford, as they will last you a lifetime if you look after them properly. (I know: I live, work and breathe by my pair of trademark orange-handled Fiskars!) Never use them to cut paper – this will blunt the blades and render them useless. To be extra sure they stay sharp, label them 'for fabric only, cut paper at your peril!' or something similar to instil terror in the hearts of scissors thieves everywhere. A small sharp pair of embroidery scissors are also indispensable for more delicate trimming and for snipping threads off finished work. And

THREAD

FUSIBLE WEBBING

FABRIC GLUE

SELF-THREADING NEEDLE

EMBROIDERY SCISSORS

FABRIC SCISSORS

QUILTING GRID MEASURE

SEWING MACHINE

THAT'S AN IDEA ...

If you're in the middle of a sewing project and can't find any dressmaking pins, try using paper clips or even hair pins (Kirby grips work great!) to keep your work safely in place.

don't forget pinking shears (scissors with zigzag teeth) – essential to create a cute non-fraying edge, super handy when you're in too much of a hurry to sew up seams and hems.

Markers   For drawing guidelines and patterns on to your fabric. There are lots to choose from. I like to use good old-fashioned tailor's chalk (chalk triangles that look like giant guitar plectrums), which can simply be brushed off fabric. I will also admit to using a soft pencil for marking fine lines on the wrong side of the fabric.

Measures   A tape measure (with both inches and centimetres) and either a quilting grid measure or a large transparent ruler are useful.

Iron   You will need an iron and an ironing board (or other flat surface) for pressing seams and finished work. A steam iron will work wonders and flatten creases where ordinary irons don't, so if you've got one, start using it now.

Seam Ripper   As ye sew, so shall ye rip! Undo erroneous stitches and wonky seams in a flash with one of these handy hookers. Simply hook the tip under a stitch and pull – your seam will unravel in seconds. Just be careful not to damage your fabric with too hasty a hand.

Pattern Paper   Square graph paper is useful for designing and marking out your own patterns – cutting fabric from a paper pattern is much more accurate and will lead to much less swearing when it comes to lining up corners or cutting out designs.

Fusible Webbing and Fabric Glue
Iron-on fusible webbing is useful for sticking down hems and bits of appliqué, and is available to buy either as a tape or in sheets – both will include a layer of protective paper to keep the adhesive from sticking to your iron. Always read the manufacturer's guidelines before using. And every seamstress needs a dab of fabric glue now and then so buy a brand that is virtually invisible when dry and works for sticking fabric to fabric as well as sticking down sequins or gems.

Sewing Machine   If you don't have one already and you're serious about stitching, it's time to start thinking about getting a sewing machine. There are machines to suit every budget and skill level (see pp. 74–5).

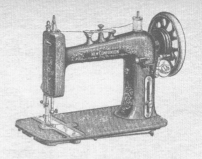

A STITCH IN TIME

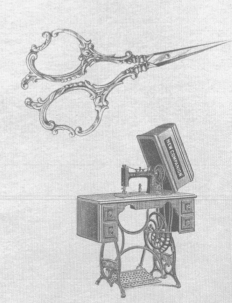

STITCH GLOSSARY

Sewing is so much simpler when you understand the lingo and getting to grips with some of the basic stitches will not only help you to better understand the making up instructions below but will also boost your confidence. So it's time to get your stitch on! Try practising on some scrap fabric first. All stitches are made from right to left unless otherwise stated, and you should always fasten off and secure thread at the end of your sewing with a couple of fix stitches (see p. 62) made to the back of the fabric.

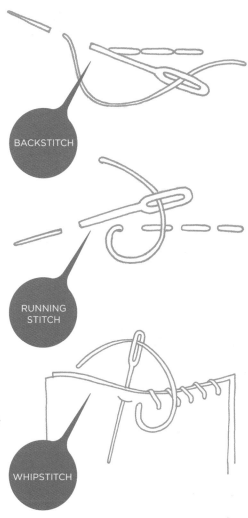

Backstitch   The most common stitch, a backstitch makes a neat line of sturdy stitches with no gaps and is primarily used for joining seams. Insert the needle from the back of the fabric to the front then, in one movement, insert it back down 3 mm along from where you just came up and back up again another 3 mm along. Now insert the needle back down against the top of the stitch you just made (this is the going-back bit) and in one movement insert the needle up 3 mm from the top of the furthest stitch. Repeat this movement to create one continuous line of overlapping stitches.

BACKSTITCH

Running Stitch   A super-fast stitch that makes a line of stitches with gaps between them used for tacking (see below) and for gathering (because the stitch is loose, you can pull on the thread and the fabric will pucker up). Insert your needle from the back of the fabric to the front, then, in one movement, insert it back down again about 3 to 6 mm along and bring it up again about the same distance along. Repeat this movement.

RUNNING STITCH

Whipstitch   A nifty little stitch worked on top of the fabric (as opposed to hidden underneath) to join two pieces together. Line up two pieces of fabric, then insert your needle from the back to the front of one piece. Now make a series of very small slanted stitches over the top edge of the two fabrics about 2 mm apart.

WHIPSTITCH

Overcast   Similar to the whipstitch above, but the stitches are made slightly bigger and further apart and are used to secure raw edges (rather than finished edges) to prevent fabric from fraying. Insert the needle from behind the two raw edges to the front of the work, then begin to make a series of evenly spaced slanted stitches about 3 mm deep and 6 mm apart.

OVERCAST

Slipstitch   This stitch is cleverly invisible from the right side of the fabric, which makes it perfect for hemming. It can also be used for anything that may be difficult to stitch on the machine, like attaching trims or finishing mitred corners (see p. 68). Insert your needle from the back to the front of the fold of your hem to hide the knot, then make a series of stitches by picking up just one or two fibres from your base fabric then inserting the needle back through the folded edge about 6 mm away (or more for bulkier fabrics) at a diagonal.

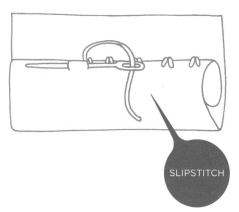

SLIPSTITCH

Blanket Stitch   One of my all-time favourite stitches, as it is functional as well as decorative. Typically used for tidying up raw edges (usually around blankets, obviously), it can also be used for stitching down appliqué and fixing fasteners like snaps and hooks and eyes. Blanket stitch is made from left to right rather than from right to left, and requires careful sewing to create a neat line. Insert the needle from the back of the fabric to the front, about 6 mm from the edge. Then insert the needle back down just to the right of where you came up. Now, before pulling the thread tight, insert your needle through the loop. Pull the thread carefully and the stitch will move up to sit along the top edge of the fabric. Continue inserting the needle from front to back and picking up the loop to create a line of linked stitches along the edge of your fabric.

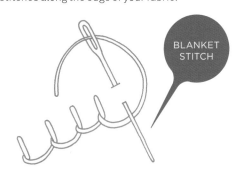

BLANKET STITCH

Fix Stitch   A fix stitch is just two or three stitches made on top of each other at the back the work to secure thread in place before and after sewing. I refer to making fix stitches all the time in this book, and this is what I mean.

FIX STITCH

Tacking   Also known as basting, tacking is a stitch used to temporarily hold pieces of fabric together before you sew them up for real. The stitches will almost always be removed after sewing so the key is to learn to work it fast and be able to remove it easily. Pin the two (or more) pieces of fabric together along the edge you want to stitch. Then thread a fine needle with some contrasting thread (that will be clearly visible against your fabric) and make a knot. Then simply sew a series of long (about 1 cm) running stitches (see above) and finish with one or two fix stitches to the back. To unpick, use a seam ripper to pull out every third or fourth stitch before unravelling. My favourite tacking technique is to make stitches even further apart (about 5–8 cm) along the seam allowance, which can then be used as a guide when stitching down permanent seams.

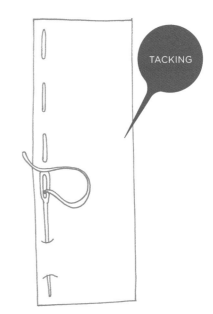

TACKING

HOW TO THREAD A NEEDLE

Choose your needle and thread to match the fabric you are working with (if your fabric is silk, use silk thread; if it's cotton, use a cotton thread). When joining dark fabric to light fabric, always use thread to match the darker fabric, as this will help your stitches appear invisible. To ensure tangle-free sewing, cut a length no longer than 50 cm and always snip at an angle (to make threading the needle just that bit easier). As a general rule, use a double thread for heavy fabrics and a single thread for light or sheer materials. To thread up, pass the thread through the eye of the needle and then pull about one third of the thread through as a tail.

*Sew out
of control*

A NEEDLEFUL OF KNOWLEDGE

Before we get stuck into the projects — and they are coming soon, I promise! — there are a few more things we need to address. Now I know we are covering a lot of ground here without much sewing going on, so I suggest that you read through these bits but don't get too bogged down. Just come back to individual instructions as and when you need them.

Preparing Fabric   Before preparing and cutting out the fabrics for your sewing projects, they must be washed and pressed to prevent your finished items from distorting when eventually laundered.

Cutting Fabric   Before measuring and marking out your fabric, you need to line your patterns or templates up against the straight lengthwise grain of the fabric. The selvedge (the non-frayed bound woven edge of the fabric) runs parallel to the lengthwise grain, so use that as your guide and simply place the patterns or templates on to the wrong side of the fabric so that they are parallel to this edge before cutting out. Always lay fabric out flat when measuring and marking out to make sure you cut accurately – a flat cutting surface and some good lighting will make all the difference. It will also be more comfortable if your cutting station or table is at standing height – constant bending down will give you a sore back.

Pinning   Always pin fabric together against the seam lines with pin heads at a perpendicular angle and to the right. This makes removing pins as you sew much easier and swifter. Place pins about 8–10 cm apart and mark out the corner seam allowances as this will help you to gauge where to pivot when sewing round corners on the machine.

Pressing   Get into the habit of pressing your work between each sewing stage to give your handmade projects a professional edge. A wise friend of my mother's once told me that a good seamstress works with a needle in one hand and an iron in the other. Pressing is a little different from everyday ironing – rather than ironing out wrinkles, you should just gently press the fabric and then lift the iron. Seams should always be pressed open flat or to one side, and always press them as you go, before they are crossed by another line of stitching.

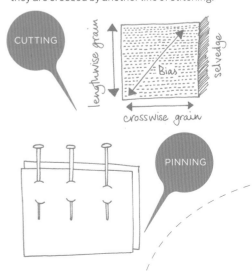

CUTTING

lengthwise grain

Bias

selvedge

crosswise grain

PINNING

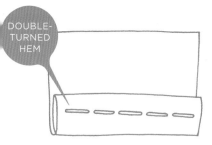

DOUBLE-TURNED HEM

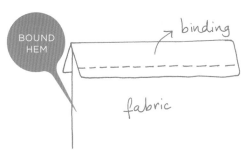

binding

fabric

BOUND HEM

How to Join a Seam   Stitch two layers of fabric together to make a seam by matching fabric edges up corner-to-corner, then either tacking or pinning in place before sewing together. Standard seam allowances can be anywhere from 2.5 cm to 6 mm. When sewing seams by hand, always use a backstitch (see p. 61) unless the instructions say otherwise. And when sewing on the machine, use a straight running stitch (see p. 61), pivoting at the corners.

How to Sew a Hem   Sewing a hem to neaten raw edges and prevent fabric from fraying is the final step to finishing off a project. Hems can either be made straight or mitred (see p. 68) at the corners. There are many ways to make a hem and which you choose will depend on your project and the fabric you are using, but for most of the projects in this book either a double-turned hem or a bound hem will do.

Double-Turned Hem   The raw edge of the fabric is turned over twice and then stitched down. First turn the fabric under 6 mm (or 1 cm if the instructions say so) to the wrong side of the work and use an iron to press the fold into place. Then turn the hem under again, this time to make up the desired hem allowance, and press before pinning or tacking into place ready to be stitched. Sew either by hand using a slipstitch (see p. 62) or on the machine with a topstitch (see p. 76), as close to the top of the fold as possible.

Bound Hem   The raw edge of the fabric is encased within a seam binding. The binding can be made from a long strip of fabric, ribbon or a specialist binding tape that is usually referred to as bias binding. The best binding tape comes ready folded (double-fold bias binding) and is the easiest to use. If you want to use ribbon (or anything else), you'll need to fold it in half along the length and press first. To sew a bound hem, encase the raw edge of the fabric inside the binding, pin and then tack the binding in place along the middle. Leave a 1 cm overhang at either end for creating a seam join. Stitch down using a topstitch on the machine (see p. 76) as close to the edge of the binding as you can and when you get to the end, fold the extra unstitched binding underneath at a diagonal, finger press, then stitch down.

GET EDGY WITH YOUR BINDINGS

As well as being functional, bindings can also be decorative and will pretty up the edges and hems of curtains, tablecloths, potholders, towels, placemats, clothing and just about anything else. Either make your own or buy ready-made binding tape. Bias binding tape is cut on the fabric's stretchiest point (the bias) and is especially useful for edging around curves. Binding tape is cut on the straight of the grain and is perfect for attaching to straight edges, like the hand towels on p. 206 or your handcrafted quilts. The finished width of most bindings can be anywhere from 6 mm to 2.5 cm on either side of the fabric. Now get edgy, have some fun and play around with the colour and the contrast of your hemline embellishments.

How to Mitre Corners   When you come to turn corners with hems, bindings or trims, you will find you have excess fabric that must be neatened and straightened out to create a clean finish. In sewing terms, this is known as mitring. When shaping bindings around corner edges, you should always attach in one continuous length.

To Mitre a Hem   Turn and press the hems under on either side of the corner to be mitred. Open the hems out again and fold the tip of the corner over using the crossing point of the hem creases you just made as a guide. Finger press, then unfold the tip. Now with right sides of the fabric facing together, fold the fabric diagonally and align the edges. Then, using a backstitch (either by hand or on the machine), stitch along the short corner crease. Snip off the corner edge 6 mm from the stitching. Turn right side out, and as the hem is folded back over the corners will naturally mitre. Just poke out the corner to get a sharp point with a blunt object like a knitting needle or a pen and press flat.

To Mitre a Flat Trim   Every trim that turns a corner must be mitred, and you'll need an extra 15 cm or so of your trimming to do it. Pin the trim in place along one edge and start stitching along the outer edge using a topstitch on the machine. Stop stitching about 2.5 cm before you get to the end, then fold the trim back on itself. Stitch a diagonal line going from the outer corner to the edge of the trim at a 45° angle. Snip off the little triangle of surplus trim close to the diagonal line you just stitched. Fold the trim back over (it should turn the corner by itself) and carry on topstitching to the next corner.

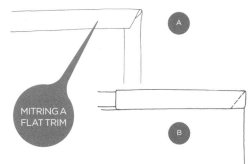

MITRING A FLAT TRIM

A

B

To Mitre a Binding   If you are using a double-fold binding tape, encase the raw edges within the centre of the binding and pin in place along one side. Start stitching along the inner edge of the binding using a topstitch on the machine, making sure you catch all three layers as you go. Stitch right to the edge, then remove the work from the machine. Fold the binding around the corner and a neat 45° angle should automatically form; pin the pleat in place. Return the work to the machine and continue stitching around the inner edge of the binding.

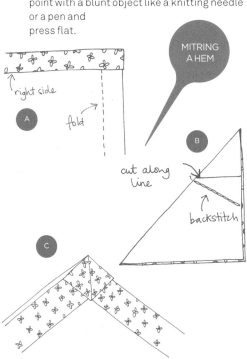

MITRING A HEM

right side

A

fold

B

cut along line

backstitch

C

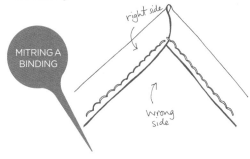

MITRING A BINDING

right side

wrong side

A Stitch in Translation

*Sometimes trying to understand sewing lingo can be
a bit like trying to translate Japanese. But don't panic!
It's super simple when you break it down. Here's some
of the most common sewing terms explained:*

BIAS
Describes the stretchiest direction of the fabric, at a 45° angle to the selvedge.

BINDING
A folded strip of fabric that encases the raw edges of another piece of fabric.

FIX STITCHING
Sewing two or three stitches on top of each other to secure a line of sewing.

GRAIN
The direction of the fabric that runs parallel to the selvedge.

HEM
The turned-under edge of the fabric that is sewn down.

MITRE
To finish a corner by stitching adjoining sides of fabric together at a 45° angle.

PRESS
Use an iron to lightly press fabric (not to smooth out wrinkles) without distorting it.

RIGHT SIDE
The side of the fabric that will face outwards once the piece is sewn up (sometimes the right side is not obvious so you have to decide which way round to use the fabric, then remember to stick to it).

SEAM
The join where two pieces of fabric are sewn together.

SEAM ALLOWANCE
The extra material that lies between the raw cut edge of the fabric and the stitching line. Standard seam allowances are usually between 6 mm and 1 cm.

SELVEDGE
The bound raw edge of the fabric bolt, where the manufacturers print their information.

TACKING
A series of long temporary stitches that hold two pieces of fabric in place before sewing.

WRONG SIDE
The reverse side of the fabric, which will face inwards once the piece is sewn up.

HEY HO! LET'S SEW!

Okay, so now it's time to put your needles to the test. Beginners should start small and try out a simple hand-sewing project like one of these pretty felt pincushions, then graduate to a nifty needle book to pop your pins in. This should build your confidence enough to try out either the quilted laptop case or the knitting bag.

These projects can be sewn either by hand or on the machine, using a dab of fabric glue here and there to secure the smaller pieces.

FAKE CAKE PINCUSHION

Fake Cake Pincushion

These pretty cake pincushions (the pins double up as decorative sprinkles) are constructed around a piece of foam, which you can buy cut to shape from a foam shop or a builder's merchant. Make your templates by drawing around your piece of foam. Now give it a go – it's a piece of cake!

YOU WILL NEED:
- For a whole cake: foam round (15 cm diameter, 9 cm high); for a cake slice: foam slice (9 cm deep and 9 cm high)
- Paper templates
- Felt scraps in cake-like colours (make sure you use heavy felt so your cushion will stand all that pin poking)
- Scissors
- Decorative ribbon, ric rac or braiding
- Needle and thread
- Glass-headed pins to decorate

MAKING:

1. Use your templates to mark out and then cut out all your felt pieces (you'll need two circles and one long strip for the whole cake, or two triangles and two rectangles for the cake slice). If you're making the whole cake, join one of the circles to the long strip using a whipstitch or blanket stitch, leaving the other circle aside. If you're making the cake slice, join the top triangle to the two rectangles and leave the bottom triangle aside. Sew these bottom pieces on last as the stitching will be visible – it can be covered up with some trimmings after you have completed step 2 and sewn on the icing.

2. To make the icing that sits around the middle of the cake, cut a long strip of ric rac or other braiding (about 50 cm) and use a backstitch to stitch it on to a 2.5 – 5 cm-wide strip of contrasting fabric, felt or ribbon. Now stitch the decorated strip around the middle of your cake or cake slice, either with a hand-sewn backstitch or a straight stitch on the machine.

CAKE SLICE PINCUSHION

DOUGHNUT PINCUSHION

Doughnut Pincushion

This doughnut pincushion only requires a handful of cotton wool or polyester stuffing to fill. Make sure the ring is deep enough to hold a pin.

YOU WILL NEED:
- A circle template or something round to draw around (a CD is perfect)
- Felt in two contrasting colours
- Scissors
- Needle and matching thread
- Small amount of polyester stuffing
- Glass-headed pins to decorate

MAKING:

1. Cut out two identical felt circles. Draw freehand on the contrasting coloured felt a splodge of icing, as wide in places as the circumference of the felt circles. With matching thread, whipstitch the icing into place on the front of one of the felt circles.

2. Place the second circle of felt behind the first and pin into place. Then from the centre point of the felt sandwich mark out a hole 2.5 cm in diameter and cut it out (this will be the hole in the middle of the doughnut).

3. Overcast the two layers together around the inner hole with matching thread. Now overcast the outer edge leaving a 2.5 cm opening. Fill the doughnut ring firmly with stuffing but be careful not to pack it too tight as the felt may rip or come apart at the seams. Then sew up the gap using an overcast stitch. Finally, add glass-headed pins to the top of the ring to create a sprinkled effect.

3. To make icing swirls for the top, cut out an 8 cm-diameter felt circle. Fold in half twice and make a stitch to the bottom to hold in place, before stitching on to your cake.

4. To make rosette icing, cut out an 8-pointed felt star with a 2.5 cm-wide base. Stitch up the sides of the star points until they all meet up, open up slightly to stuff with a tiny bit of cotton wool or polyester stuffing, then secure with a stitch before stitching (or gluing) on to your cake.

5. To make strawberries, cut out a semicircle of red felt, fold it in half and sew up the straight edge with a whipstitch. Turn the right way round, stitch a running stitch around the top edge of the cone and pull on the thread to gather closed. Open up slightly, stuff and then secure the top with a few stitches. Now cut out a 4-pointed stem shape from a scrap of green felt. Make a fix stitch on the top of the strawberry and bring the needle through the centre of the stem. Stitch the stem down on to the strawberry, catching each point of the leaves before fastening off. Attach the strawberries to the cake with a stitch, some glue or just a well-positioned pin.

Needle Book

This practical and pretty needle book makes an adorable hand-sewn gift to give to fellow stitch queens and can be personalized accordingly. Decorate with appliqué, embroidery, studs or pins. You could even embellish it with an old badge collection or the initials of your friend. You'll need some thin wadding for this project.

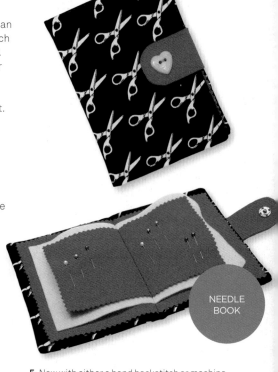

NEEDLE BOOK

YOU WILL NEED:
- 2 x fabric rectangles, 25 x 18 cm
- 1 x wadding rectangle, 25 x 18 cm
- 3 x felt rectangles, 23 x 16 cm
- 2 x felt rectangles, 4 x 5 cm, for tab closure
- 1 pair of fastener snaps
- Rhinestone gem or button for decorating
- Pins
- Tape measure
- Pinking shears
- Needle and matching thread
- Sewing machine (optional)
- Fabric glue

MAKING:

1. Place one of the fabric rectangles on top of the wadding rectangle with right side facing up and corners aligned. Then place the second fabric rectangle over the first with wrong side facing up. Pin or tack the three pieces together.

2. Stitch around the edges, either by hand using a backstitch or on the machine with a straight running stitch and a 1 cm seam allowance, leaving an 8 cm opening in the middle of one of the short sides of the rectangle.

3. Trim off any excess and snip each corner before turning right side out. Poke out the corners to sharp points with a pencil or a knitting needle before pressing and removing any tacks. Press in half to create a booklet, making sure you tuck in and press the seam allowance neatly at the seam opening – this is where you will sew in the tab closure.

4. To make the tab closure, hold the two small felt rectangles together and round off one short end with some scissors. Then sew them either by hand using a backstitch or on the machine with a top stitch. Now insert the square end of the tab closure into the 8 cm seam opening, folding the seam allowance under to neaten, and pin into place.

5. Now with either a hand backstitch or machine topstitch, sew around the entire fabric rectangle about 6 mm from the edge, catching the tab closure and open seam as you stitch. Press, then fold the rectangle in half and press again to create a spine crease.

6. To make the felt pages to sit inside, trim the edges of one of your felt rectangles with pinking shears so that it is 1 cm smaller on all sides than your needle book. Now trim another felt rectangle in a corresponding colour, and this time make it 1 cm smaller again on all sides. Finally, trim a third felt rectangle 2.5 cm smaller again. Place the three felt rectangles together with the largest on the bottom and the smallest on the top, pin them into place and sew along the centrefold of the needle book spine.

7. To add the fastener to the tab closure, mark out its position first, making sure the socket will meet the ball when closed. Then use a matching thread to sew each loop of the snap into place (see box, below), catching just the top layer of fabric.

8. For some extra sparkle, attach a rhinestone gem or a fancy button with some fabric glue. Leave to dry before filling the book with pins and needles.

HEY HO
LETS
SEW

MAY YOUR BOBBIN ALWAYS BE FULL — TIPS ON BUYING AND USING A SEWING MACHINE

If you're serious about sewing, then it may be well worth investing in a sewing machine. Even if you don't expect to be stitching couture or sewing free-hand embroidery, it will make all those smaller jobs (not to mention long seams and hems) just that bit easier. The good news is that you don't have to spend lots of money – there are models on the market to suit any budget.

IT'S A SNAP — HOW TO SEW ON A SNAP FASTENER

Mark out where you want your snaps to be on your fabric with a marker. Make sure that the socket will meet the ball when closed. Then use a matching thread and a blanket stitch to sew each loop of the snap into place.

You should buy the best you can afford, so figure out your budget and then stick to it. It's only worth stretching if you seriously plan on getting a lot of use out of your machine and want access to all the fancy functions that come with top-end models. My first sewing machine was a hand-me-down from my mum – a 1970s Frister & Rossmann beauty in beige. Although it had been a much-loved 16th birthday present to my mum, to me it was bulky, old-fashioned and, worst of all, unfriendly. It never let me sew my seams straight and I always ended up in a mass of tangled thread. Even so, it's been repaired over and over and is still part of the family. Lesson: your machine may well be with you for a lifetime, so it's worth spending money on this all-important purchase. But be realistic about your own skill level and what you think you might want to use your machine for: if you buy something too complicated to use, it will just end up at the back of a cupboard. All you really need is a sturdy machine that is easy to use and has a few extra stitch functions (like zigzag and satin stitch).

Where and What to Buy For a new machine, check out your local sewing machine dealer first. Not only will you get one-to-one service, you'll also be able to try machines out and know that you can go back to the shop if anything goes wrong. Department stores like John Lewis can also be good places to look at a variety of different models and get advice from experts, and they offer free half-hour sewing lessons to those interested in road-testing their machines too. Otherwise, scour your local paper for second-hand – you might find yourself a bargain.

Wherever your machine comes from, make sure you buy a well-established brand so that spare parts and accessories will be easy to get hold of in the future. Singer and Janome both make excellent machines – my favourite is the Janome 2522LE, a really reliable mid-range model that has all the functions you'll need without being mega complicated and scary. It will last a lifetime of stitches.

A Girl's Best Friend   Okay, now you've got your marvellous machine, it's time to get acquainted. First things first, read your manual cover to cover. Yes, this may sound boring and yes, I'm sure your fingers are burning to just start sewing, but it will save a lot of frustration and unpicking in the long run if you work out what all the twiddly knobs and buttons do first. And remember, sewing can be dangerous. Don't giggle, it's true! And I should know – I've been at the wrong end of many a rookie mistake. Once, I was over-enthusiastically trying to sew several heavy layers of denim with the wrong needle, because I was in a hurry and desperate to get my jeans turned up quickly. Big mistake. I rammed my foot down on the pedal (thinking that if I just did it quickly maybe the machine wouldn't notice) when bang! The needle snapped, came flying towards my face and pinged off my forehead. Now although I was only left with a sting, I was shocked enough to start paying my machine more respect. So make friends with your machine and it will be friends with you.

NOVELTY MACHINES

If you want some sewing speed and only have a few quid to spare, consider purchasing a cheap novelty sewing machine. You won't be able to master all the tricks of the trade with one of these little cuties, but they are fine for beginners who want to learn on something fun and non-threatening before they gain the confidence to move up to a more complicated machine. My favourite novelty machine comes from John Lewis, and is stocked in a range of pretty pastels and bright candy neons (see 'Address Book', p. 234). I use mine as a portable to take to sewing meets.

NEVER LET YOUR SEWING MACHINE KNOW YOU'RE IN A HURRY

— *Pay attention to tension. Tension regulates the stitches and is usually controlled by turning a dial on the front of the machine. If the tension is set too tight, the stitches will bunch up and break. If the tension is set too loose, the stitches will not hold.*

— *Play the long game. The length of the stitch determines the stitch's durability so make sure you adjust the stitch length accordingly. Short stitches are very strong and are meant to be permanent, while longer stitches are usually temporary or are used as a decorative topstitch. When sewing anything other than straight stitch, you also need to pay attention to stitch width, which controls the distance the needle moves from side to side when making a stitch.*

— *Give your needle a break. As with hand sewing, you need different needles to sew different fabrics. As I learnt the hard way, you can't sew over layers of heavy denim with a regular needle, and instead must invest in a special denim needle for the job. Needles will blunt over time too, so replace them regularly.*

— *Sew straight. Hear me out on this one. Learning to sew straight lines will build your confidence and help you understand the rhythm of your machine. So practise, practise, practise.*

— *Follow the leader. Always keep the fabric aligned with the marking lines on the throat plate (the metal plate that sits below the needle and presser foot) and make sure you watch the marking lines as you sew, not the fabric.*

Machine Stitches

Straight stitch The most basic machine stitch, straight stitch makes a neat line of identical straight stitches. Use your length control to lengthen or shorten the stitch.

Zigzag stitch Use this stitch to neaten raw edges and prevent fraying. Perfect for appliqué. Use the controls to alter both the length and width of the zigzag.

Satin stitch A very close zigzag stitch used for neatening and covering raw edges.

Topstitch A straight stitch used for finishing hems, topstitch creates a firm stable edge as well as keeping layers of fabric together.

MACHINE QUILTING

Adding a layer of wadding to your work and sewing over the top of the fabric is called quilting, and besides providing protective padding it also looks very pretty. It's simple to sew as long as you use a lightweight wadding (see p. 57).

Before moving to the machine, make sure you tack your fabric and wadding layers together first as the bulkiness of the fabric will cause it to shift about as you sew. Loosen the tension on your sewing machine and set to a long straight stitch, then beginning at the centre and working your way out towards the edge (this will help stop bulking), just feed the fabric–wadding sandwich through the machine, stitching down in either diagonal or parallel lines. The most popular quilting designs are diagonal quilting, square quilting and channel quilting (made up from parallel rows of stitching). And I love them all! They're all super easy to sew, so just see how the mood takes you and experiment with what works best.

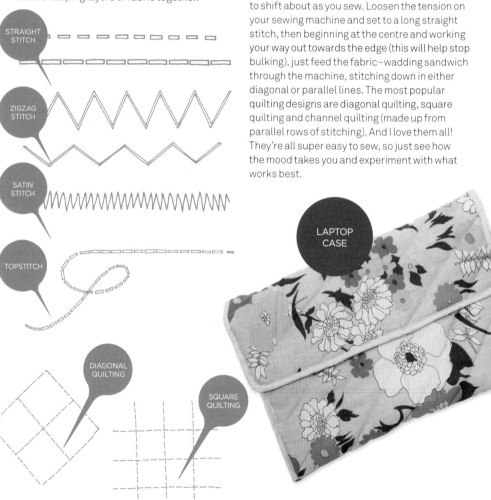

STRAIGHT STITCH

ZIGZAG STITCH

SATIN STITCH

TOPSTITCH

LAPTOP CASE

DIAGONAL QUILTING

SQUARE QUILTING

Quilted Potholder

Freshen up your kitchen with these hot-stuff fruit-themed quilted potholders. Make sure your fabric, binding and wadding is machine washable, as your potholders are likely to get dirty over time.

QUILTED POTHOLDER

YOU WILL NEED:
- 2 x fabric squares, 19 x 19 cm
- 1 x wadding square, 20 x 20 cm
- 90 cm of 20 mm double-fold binding tape
- Sewing machine
- Matching threads
- Pins

MAKING:

1. Sandwich the wadding in between the two squares of fabric with right sides facing out and pin in place.

2. Loosen the tension on your sewing machine and set to a long straight stitch, then stitch a diagonal line from one corner to the other, then sew the opposite diagonal. Turn around and sew back in the opposite direction, creating a diagonal grid of lines at regular intervals. Trim any untidy edges and loose threads.

3. Pin the binding in place, mitring the corners as you go, and sew down using a topstitch as close to the binding edge as you can, making sure it is level on both sides. Fold the excess binding in half to create a loop and stitch down to secure.

Laptop Case

Pretty laptop cases are notoriously hard to come by. But I have a friend who carries hers around in a vintage pyjama case, which inspired me to design my own version. A spot of machine quilting will be needed to pad out the case, but it's simple so don't worry. This case will fit a 13-inch laptop.

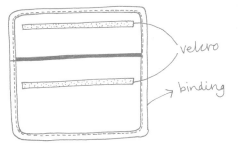

velcro

binding

YOU WILL NEED:
- 2 x fabric rectangles, 71 x 41 cm
- 1 x wadding rectangle, 76 x 46 cm
- 190 cm of 25 mm double-fold binding tape
- 36 cm strip of Velcro
- Sewing machine
- Matching threads
- Pins

MAKING:

1. Along one of the shorter sides of one of the fabric rectangles, sew the hooked strip of the Velcro on to the right side of the fabric 1.5 cm from the edge, using a straight stitch on the machine.

2. Sandwich the wadding in between the two squares of fabric with right sides facing out and pin in place.

3. Loosen the tension on your machine, set to a long straight stitch and, starting in the centre, stitch diagonal lines at regular intervals, making sure you smooth any wrinkles out of the fabric as you sew. Trim any untidy edges and loose threads.

4. Attach the loop strip of the Velcro on the opposite side and end of the quilt sandwich, 9 cm down from the top edge, and sew it across the width of the quilt sandwich. Then encase the raw edge width directly above with a strip of double-fold binding tape and topstitch into place.

5. Turn this end up to make a 25 cm fold and pin in place. Your laptop will eventually sit inside this envelope.

6. Pin the binding in place around all three raw edges, mitring the corners as you go. Sew down using a topstitch close to the binding edge, making sure it is level on both sides. Stop stitching about 2.5 cm before the end of the binding, fold the raw edge under 1 cm and stitch to the end.

Knitting and Sewing Bag

Stitch up your own knitting or needlework bag to carry your crafty supplies around town. Just grab yourself a pair of handles: haberdasheries usually sell a good selection of plastic, wooden, bamboo and even sparkly ones.

YOU WILL NEED:
- Fabric rectangle, 91 x 56 cm
- 1 pair of handles
- Matching threads
- Sewing machine
- Pins

MAKING:

1. Fold the fabric rectangle in half widthwise with wrong sides together. Pin the side seams, stopping when you get about a quarter of the way from the top, then stitch down using a straight stitch.

2. Trim off a triangle from the point where you stopped stitching to the top edge at a 45° angle on both sides. Turn down a 6 mm seam, press and stitch down using a straight stitch.

3. Fold the top edges over 6 mm on to the wrong side of the fabric on both sides and press.

4. Turn the work the right way round and get your handles ready. Fold the top seam on one side over the handle and pin in place. Use a slipstitch to sew the seam with the 6mm pressed hem down on to the wrong side of the fabric. The fabric should gather around the handle as you stitch. Repeat for the other handle.

LAPTOP CASE

YO-YO PATCHES

Yo-yo patches are little gathered circles of fabric that can be either sewn together or used individually for pretty appliqué decoration. They are extremely simple to make and a great way to use up fabric scraps, and they make the most adorable embellishments on clothing, blankets, tablecloths and accessories.

2. When you get to the end, carefully pull the thread to gather the fabric up into a puff shape. Knot the thread and secure the ends inside.

3. Ease into shape with your hands, pressing the yo-yo flat. The side with the gathering is the right side of the work. Add a bit of polyester stuffing to enhance the shape if you fancy and sew a bead or button at the centre to embellish.

Yo-Yo Flower Power   Now have a go at making a simple fabric flower by placing a small yo-yo patch on top of a larger one and sewing together in the centre, adding a decorative button or a pretty bead. Add a pin to the back to make a brooch, attach with a dab of glue to a hair clip, or make a few and glue them all along an old hairband.

How to Make a Yo-Yo

First you need to make a circular paper template twice the diameter of the finished yo-yo plus an extra 6 mm for turning the seam. For a large yo-yo patch, try a circle template 9 cm in diameter, and for a smaller yo-yo, try a 4 cm-diameter template. Then you only need a scrap of fabric – lightweight cottons and silks work the best; avoid very heavy fabrics as they won't gather into pretty little puffs – and some matching thread.

YOU WILL NEED:
• Circular template
• Scrap fabric
• Fabric scissors
• Needle and matching thread
• Polyester stuffing (optional)
• Bead or button to embellish (optional)

MAKING:

1. Using your template, cut out your fabric circle. Turn about 6 mm of the outer edge of the circle down on to the wrong side of the fabric. Make a knot in your thread, bring the needle up from back to front and sew running stitches around the circumference of the circle.

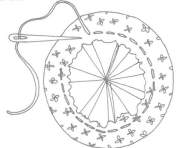

YO-YO ON THE GO

Yo-yo patches are the perfect travel-size project for stitching on the train or while waiting for the bus. Most craft shops sell plastic yo-yo maker kits, which come in a variety of different shapes and sizes including hearts, petals and even butterflies. They are easy to use – just press a square of fabric on to the plastic yo-yo holder, then trim leaving a scant hem and sew through the little holes around the edge before removing the fabric from the holder, gathering up the circle and securing with a knot. This makes the stitching up so much easier for you to yo-yo on the go!

Yo-Yo Garland   Bright multi-coloured patches strung together in a garland will brighten up any room or party. I have a special thing for polka dot yo-yo garlands, but why not make festive-themed garlands for the holidays or personalize handmade gifts for friends? To make one metre of yo-yo garland with a finished patch size of 6 cm you will need to make at least 16 patches. Link them with strong linen thread as follows: put two patches together, gathered sides facing in, and join their edges with four small whipstitches very close together. Secure with a backstitch. Continue adding patches until they are all joined.

PATCHWORK

PATCH WORK

The word 'patchwork' describes the craft almost perfectly: the age-old practice of piecing together scrap patches of fabric andthen sewing them (either by hand or using the machine) edge-to-edge to create decorative designs. Patchwork is not to be confused with its sister craft, quilting: stitching decorative outlines and patterns on to layers of fabric (see pp. 76—7 for a quilted laptop case and hot-stuff potholders). However, the two crafts are often done together, as you will find out if you try your hand at making my neon Thunderbird patchwork quilt on p. 98. Piecing patchwork is a fun way to jazz up a space and you can play around and experiment with a dizzying array of colours and geometric designs while keeping a timeworn tradition alive.

BACK TO SQUARE ONE

Like most other needlecrafts, patchwork
originally came about through thrift.
Considered to be one of the earliest
crafts, patchwork was practised,
in primitive form, in ancient Egypt.
And it's easy to understand why it's
been around so long when you consider
that the need to repair damaged
garments has been a universal problem
for centuries.

Salvaging scrap materials to be repieced and sewn into new patches of fabric was part of good old-fashioned domestic ingenuity, and to this day it remains one of the most economical crafts as it can be worked almost entirely from scrap materials – lucky if you're anything like me and hold on to every tattered shred you've ever come across. (I even have a scrap bag where I house the tiniest of treasured threads.)

Patchwork only really began to take off as a craft in the nineteenth century at the onset of the industrial revolution, which brought with it a rush of affordable fabrics. Beautiful imported Indian chintz and Persian silks were newly available and so it became a popular pastime for gentlewomen of leisure. But it was in America that patchwork really hit the big time, brought over by European colonists whose pioneer spirit began the great American tradition of patchwork quilting. 'Quilting bees' started here too; local women would come together to exchange stories, skills and gossip. These social gatherings were popular not only because of the friendships made over the hoops but also because with patchwork, the old adage 'many hands make light work' really does ring true. As a teenybopper, I used to watch Winona Ryder in *How to Make an American Quilt* over and over again, dreaming about one day learning to quilt while sharing stories with my friends. And getting involved with the Shoreditch Sisters finally gave me my chance – see p. 220 for my tips on how to start your own quilting club.

Today, patchwork and quilting have really started to take off again among a new generation who are finding more and more reasons to gather together and stitch. And for almost every event or occasion, there is a patchwork quilt that can be made to mark it – you could get together with a group of friends and sew a friendship quilt, or make a marriage quilt for a touching and thoughtful wedding gift. Or get granny on board and stitch a family heirloom quilt. This was how I first learnt to piece patchwork – my granny discovered an unfinished quilt that had been started by her mother lying mouldering in the attic and we decided to join forces and finish it. It warms my heart whenever I look at it and think of those precious hours spent stitching with my granny. I love this unique ability of patchwork to chronicle personal histories, immortalized in the weave of the fabric. Especially if the patchwork is built up with fabrics that hold personal significance, like the squares of faded but well-loved childhood dresses that my granny and I sewed into our quilt. Patchwork is ideal for preserving these kinds of materials and because of this is often described as one of the most sentimental needlecrafts – precious mementos can be created out of even the scrappiest of tattered treasures.

Though a deeply traditional craft, patchwork can also be thoroughly modern and subversive. And no one has done it better or with more guts than Tracey Emin, whose provocatively appliquéd and patchworked fabric installations are made up of confessional hand-stitched messages and symbols. This experimental, exciting approach to an ancient craft should get your hands twitching – you too can throw caution to the wind and run riot planning your own crazy creations.

Stitching a patchwork quilt from scratch is a slow and time-consuming process, and while it's well worth the effort in the long run, my advice for beginners is to start small. So to road-test your skills, why not try stitching a snazzy nine-patch pillow (see p. 97) or hand-piecing a pretty hexagon pincushion (p. 93)? Learning patchwork techniques is easy, and once you've mastered just a few basic principles, you'll soon find yourself immersed in a kaleidoscopic world of infinite invention.

SQUARE ONE

EQUIPMENT

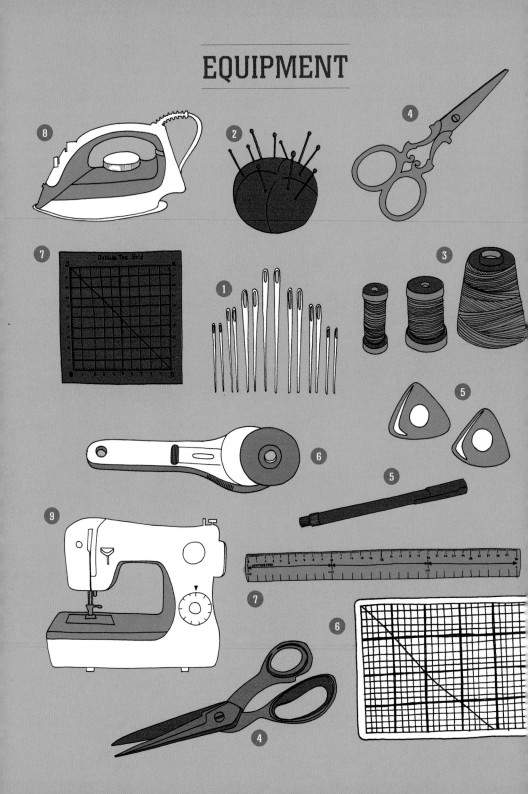

Quilters Never Cut Corners

Patchwork is a needlecraft that relies on precision, so having the right equipment is vital if you want to make something that looks good and will stand the test of time. The good news is that you probably have most of these basic tools in your stash already – apart from the templates and papers, which you can either make by hand or buy from a specialist shop or online.

TOOLS AND MATERIALS

1. Needles

Fine, sharp, short needles are best for hand sewing patchwork pieces together, to ensure your stitches are neat and closely joined. Needles come in sizes ranging from 1 to 10 (10 being the shortest and finest, 1 being the thickest and longest); 9 and 10 are best for patchwork. But I also like to use 'self-threading' needles – true time-savers, as the thread simply pops on and off the eye of the needle, which makes the fiddly parts of hand sewing much less, well, fiddly.

2. Pins

There's nothing more frustrating than a blunt pin at a crucial sewing moment, so your pins must be super sharp. Steel dressmaking pins are best and if you can find some with large pearl or glass heads, so much the better for securing larger patchwork blocks. Keep an eye out and discard rusted pins, which will damage your fabric.

3. Thread

Strong cotton or polyester sewing thread is best. Try to match the thread to both the material you are working with (i.e., use cotton thread with cotton fabric) and the colour of your fabric – as a general rule, a darker thread is less

obvious when joining dark colours to light. To make a feature of stitches around your appliqué work, invest in decorative threads like Lurex, metallics, silks and embroidery skeins for an adventurous mix of contrasting stitches.

4. Scissors

You will need at least two pairs of scissors: a pair of paper scissors for cutting out templates and another pair of sharp fabric scissors for cutting out fabric. A smaller pair of embroidery scissors can also be useful for snipping the ends of threads. Never use the fabric scissors to cut out paper or cardboard, as this will blunt them.

5. Fabric Markers

Tailor's chalk or invisible fabric pens are useful for drawing around templates and marking out patches and seam allowance guidelines on to your fabric. If using speciality pens, always make sure you read the manufacturer's guidelines before using – and only use ones that will wash or brush out.

6. Self-Healing Mat and Rotary Cutter

Although not essential, both of these tools will make fabric cutting much quicker – the rotary cutter (a circular rotating blade that looks like a pizza slicer) can cut through several layers at once and is also useful for trimming the raw edges of finished squares and blocks. Always use a rotary cutter with a self-healing cutting mat to protect your work surface and always push the blade away from you as you cut.

7. Measures

You will need an acrylic see-through ruler or specialist quilting measure such as an Omnigrid or rotary ruler for measuring and marking out patches on to fabric.

8. Iron

You will need an iron for pressing seams and your finished work – always remember to press seams as you go for a professional finish.

9. Sewing Machine

For machine-worked patchwork. See p. 74 for advice on purchasing your first sewing machine.

TEMPLATES

To ensure all your pieces are exactly the same size and shape, you'll need a template. You can either make them yourself or buy them.

Buying Templates

Made from either metal or plastic, shop-bought templates are sturdy and long lasting. They are best sourced directly from specialist quilting shops or haberdashery stores – most should stock a good selection of shapes and sizes. You can also buy plastic window templates, with both the inner measurement for the final patch size and the outer frame, including the seam allowance, giving both the sewing and cutting guidelines. The size of the template is usually given as the length of the sides.

Making Templates

Make your own templates from stiff paper or card. The benefit of homemade templates is that they can be any size or shape you like; however, they will wear out over time and often need replacing. You can draw simple shapes freehand, trace them from patterns or, for more accurate geometric designs, use a ruler and protractor. Always make sure you cut them out as accurately as possible and, if you're making templates for machine-sewn patchwork, always include a 6 mm seam allowance.

FABRICS

Part of the fun of patchwork is in collecting fabrics and thinking about the types of colours and designs you want to work with. The possibilities really are endless. Always think carefully about how your finished project will be used and whether or not it will need to be washed, and then choose your fabrics to suit: never use fragile fabrics for something that is going to have a lot of wear.

All sorts of fabrics can be used for patchwork, including linen, silk, corduroy, velvet and even leather, but always try to combine fabrics of similar weight and thickness. For beginners, it's best to stick to non-stretch cottons or cotton–polyester mixes, as you will find these much easier to work with. Try to avoid man-made or synthetic fibres altogether, as they can be slippery to handle and it will be difficult to make accurate seams when it comes to piecing your patches together.

Always wash and iron fabrics before you use them to prevent any shrinking or colours running when your finished work is eventually washed.

THE WHOLE NINE YARDS – FINDING FABRICS

Charity shops, car boot sales and flea markets are great places to find cheap vintage materials, which look brilliant mixed in with more modern prints. However, always be careful to check for wear and tear as this will affect the overall durability of your finished work. Get into the habit of recycling and keep a scrap box to store all your off-cuts and odd remnants from other sewing projects. You can also buy fabrics for patchwork pre-measured and pre-cut in bundles. Although these can be expensive, most of the hard work (the measuring and cutting) has already been done for you. There are two types of pre-cut fabrics available:

Fat quarter Although it sounds like the street term for some sort of contraband, a fat quarter is really just a quarter of a square yard of fabric.

Jelly roll A roll of about 40–50 assorted pre-cut strips of fabric sold in a bundle ready to go.

Hand-Sewn
Patchwork

Hand sewing and machine sewing
patchwork are two very different
techniques. Unlike with other sewing
projects, it isn't always possible to
just go ahead and machine sew
patchwork that is designed to be
pieced by hand. Many classic
patchwork shapes, like the hexagon
(see p. 91), are too fiddly to be
stitched on the machine and must be
hand-pieced instead. Luckily, learning
to hand sew patchwork is simple — the
only stitching skills required are
whipstitch and tacking.

Hand-sewn patchwork is traditionally worked using a technique called paper piecing. In simple terms, this just means that every piece of fabric is tacked or basted (sewn with large removable stitches; see p. 63) on to a paper counterpart (to help keep the fabric pieces a uniform shape and size), which is sewn into the design and then removed once the final stitches have been made.

The use of scrap paper has long been a part of traditional patchwork economizing so raid the house for junk mail, glossy magazines and old letters. The paper should be firm enough to be felt through the fold of the fabric but not as thick as card, which would be difficult to handle. Keep in mind that you will eventually have to remove the paper patches before lining and backing. (Many years ago, before the luxury of central heating, the paper patches were kept inside the patchwork and sewn up into the finished work to add an extra layer of warmth. And for a romantic touch, so the stories go, the papers used were often personal mementos and treasured keepsakes.) Like your fabric pieces, these paper pieces are cut from the master template and must be cut as accurately as possible. If you have one, a craft knife will give the best results, though paper scissors will do.

FLOWER POWER PATCHWORK

One of the most common and well-loved hand-pieced patchwork designs, hexagons experienced a massive boom in popularity during the 60s and 70s, as rainbow-hued patchworks became part of the swirling psychedelic landscape. Today, it remains a vintage classic and can be worked into just about anything: think flower power bedspreads, bright pastel print appliqué cushions and bold retro embellishments.

To work hexagon patchwork, individual hexagon patches are first basted on to paper templates, then folded and sewn edge-to-edge to build up a mosaic of colour. The repetitive work of hand sewing the patches together is an ideal down-time activity to be done while relaxing in front of the TV or even on the go – the perfect handbag-size project. Before you embark on one of the following projects, practise making a single rosette (see p. 92). Attach it to the side of a bag or on the pocket of your jeans, or chintz up a cushion.

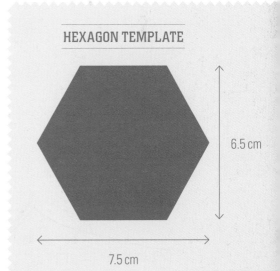

HEXAGON TEMPLATE

6.5 cm

7.5 cm

HOW TO MAKE A PATCHWORK ROSETTE

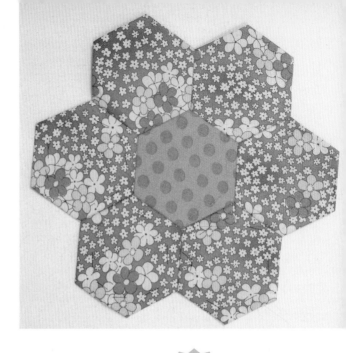

A rosette consists of six hexagons sewn around a central hexagon. For a larger rosette, an additional ring of twelve can also be added in another contrasting colour or print. Remember that precision is key: if your patches are uneven, your work will not lie flat.

You will need:
- Hexagon template (see p. 91)
- Paper
- Scrap fabric
- Fabric and paper scissors (or a craft knife)
- Needle and matching thread
- Iron

Making:

1. Cutting the paper patches
Use the master template to cut out the required number of paper patches (7 for a small rosette, 19 for a large one) using either a sharp pair of scissors or a craft knife.

2. Cutting the fabric patches
Cut out the required number of square fabric patches. They should be 1 cm wider than the hexagon on all sides.

3. Basting Pin the paper patches to the centre of the wrong side of the fabric patches. Carefully fold one of the fabric sides over the edge of the paper. With a small knot in your thread, insert your needle from the front of the fabric through to the back of the paper and tack the turned edge in place using a long running stitch (see p. 61). Fold the next edge over, as close to the paper as possible, and keep going with your running stitch to tack in place. Carry on folding the edges and tacking in place until all the sides are turned, finishing with an extra stitch at the end to keep the thread in place. Repeat for all patches.

4. Joining the patches Take the centre patch and put it together with one of the outside patches with right sides facing (the paper sides will be facing out) and corners aligned. Working from left to right, use a whipstitch (see p. 61) to join the edges with short neat stitches. As you work from corner to corner, be sure to pick up only a small amount of fabric as you go along and do not sew through the papers. To attach the next patch, position it in place against the other two seams, keeping the corners aligned, and whipstitch the edges as before. Continue adding patches in this way until the rosette is complete.

5. Finishing Unpick the tacking stitches then press the work on the wrong side. Remove the papers; if any are still intact, they can be used again.

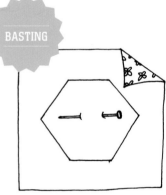

BASTING

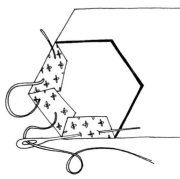

NEON CHINTZ PINCUSHION

An ideal project for beginners who need to gain confidence, this patched pincushion uses the classic 'Grandmother's Flower Garden' design (i.e., the rosette you just made above) but brings it bang up to date by replacing traditional florals with riotous neon chintz. Raid your scrap box and use up any old remnants of fabric to mix and match prints.

The pincushion is pieced in two halves, with both a front and back flower rosette. Remember – accuracy is key!

You will need:
- Hexagon template (see p. 91)
- Paper
- Scrap fabric – non-stretch cottons work best and preferably something with a bit of durability
- Fabric and paper scissors (or a craft knife)
- Needle and matching thread
- Iron
- Polyester stuffing

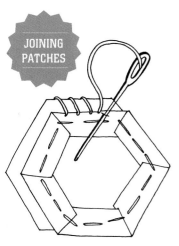

JOINING PATCHES

Making:

1. Cutting the paper patches Cut out 14 paper patches (7 for the front and 7 for the back).

2. Cutting the fabric patches Now cut out 14 fabric patches, making sure they are 1 cm wider than the paper hexagons.

3. Basting Pin the paper templates on to the centre of the wrong side of each of the fabric patches and fold over and tack the edges of each one around the paper hexagons (as for the single rosette).

4. Joining the patches Begin joining the patches together to make the first rosette. Take one of your centre patches and one of the outside patches and hold them together with right sides facing each other and the paper sides facing out. With neat short stitches, oversew both edges from corner to corner with a whipstitch. Continue joining patches around the centre hexagon until all seams are joined and the work resembles a flower. This is your first rosette patch. Repeat for the second rosette.

5. Joining the two rosettes With right sides facing each other and papers on the outside, match up the corners of the two rosettes and whipstitch the edges, leaving all but one seam free.

6. Finishing Unpick the tacking stitches, press and remove the papers. Turn right side out, using a pencil or knitting needle to work out the corners. Stuff the pincushion firmly, making sure all the corners are well filled. Finally, whipstitch the open seam shut.

ROSETTE CUSHION COVER

Pretty up a dull cushion cover with a large patchwork rosette. If you don't already have a cushion cover ready to revamp, consider making your own – it's easy.

You will need:
- Hexagon template (p. 91)
- Paper
- Scrap fabrics
- Fabric and paper scissors (or craft knife)
- Needle and matching thread
- Iron
- Cushion cover

Making:

1. Make a large patchwork rosette using 19 hexagon patches (see p. 92)

2. Remove the tacking stitches, press and remove the papers.

3. Use a whipstitch to sew the rosette on to your cushion cover.

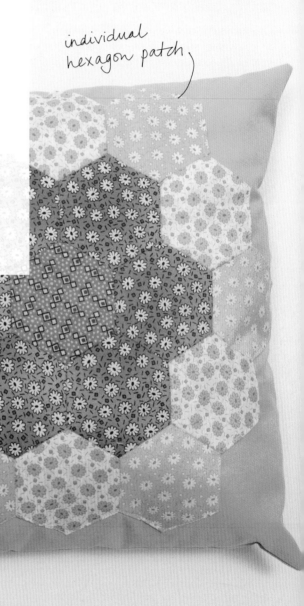

individual hexagon patch

FLOWER POWER QUILT

Now go one step further and make a flower power bed quilt to go with your rosette cushion. A word of advice when you're choosing your fabrics: this is a large-scale project and you don't want your finished quilt to give you a headache! So consider the colours and patterns of your fabrics carefully. Think about the balance of light and dark and the final positioning within the design. Try picking a colour theme and then find as many fabrics as you can in varying shades, mixing plain and prints to play with perspective and create eye-catching effects.

QUILT TEMPLATE

approx 75 cm

approx 125 cm

You will need:
- Hexagon template, 5 cm wide (includes seam allowance)
- Scrap paper
- Scrap fabric
- Fabric and paper scissors (or craft knife)
- Needle and matching thread
- Fabric backing, 152 x 76 cm
- Cotton interlining, 152 x 76 cm
- 471 cm (the sum of the edges plus 15 cm extra) 6–9 cm double-fold binding
- Iron
- Sewing machine (optional)

Making:
1. Make the rosettes Using the instructions on p. 92, make up 26 rosettes plus a few extra single hexagon patches.

2. Piece the rosettes Lay the rosettes out on a large flat surface and position and reposition until you have a design you are happy with. Piece the rosettes together in strips. Then piece the strips together. Use the extra single hexagons to piece in the gaps around the edge. Undo all the tacking stitches and remove the papers from all the hexagons except those around the edge of the quilt. Press the quilt to neaten.

3. Finishing Place the hexagon quilt top right side down against the work surface. Then place the rectangle of cotton interlining on top and the rectangle of backing fabric on top of this. Line up the edges so the quilt top fits perfectly within the rectangle and pin together. Then carefully trim the hexagon quilt top to match the other two layers. Now tack around the edges of the fabric sandwich, removing any leftover papers from the quilt top, before sewing into place 6 mm from the edge with a hand-sewn backstitch or using a straight stitch on the machine.

4. Binding Pin the binding in place around the quilt, starting in the middle of one edge and mitring the corners as you go (see p. 68). Then, either by hand using a slipstitch (see p. 62) or on the machine using a topstitch (see p. 76), sew down close to the edge of the binding, being sure to stitch through all three layers as you go. Stop stitching about 2.5 cm before the end of the binding, fold the raw edge under 1 cm and stitch to the end.

Machine-Sewn Patchwork – Hip to Be Square

Machine patchwork is worked in quite a different way from hand-sewn patchwork. Usually, square or rectangular patches are sewn together into long strips, and these strips are sewn together to finish (hence machine patchwork is sometimes called 'strip piecing'). Naturally, it is a much faster way of making patchwork than hand sewing and, though the designs you can build with only squares and rectangles are limited, some skilful use of colour and pattern can really bring machine patchwork to life.

HOW TO PIECE PATCHWORK SQUARES

You can make your square template by hand or use a shop-bought one. If you decide to make yours, remember to include a 6 mm seam allowance on all sides. Once you have your template ready, you can start piecing your squares:

1. Cutting the patches Using your template, cut out the desired number of fabric patches. Always cut along the straight grain of the fabric (see p. 66) and mark out your 6 mm seam allowances on to the wrong side of each fabric square using a ruler and some tailor's chalk. Press all the patches.

2. Positioning On a flat surface (I often use the floor), build up a design with your squares, thinking carefully about colour and pattern. Remember, your patches will be sewn in strips, so think about which column or row you plan to join together first.

3. Sewing the strips Take two patches and align them with right sides facing. Using a straight stitch on the machine (see p. 76), join them together along the

marked-out seam line. Now take another patch and join it to one of the two patches you have just joined. Keep adding patches to the strip until one column or row of your design is complete. Repeat for the rest and press all the finished strips.

4. Joining the strips With right sides facing, pin two of the strips together, matching up all the corners of the individual patches. Try to be as accurate as you can here – you may have to tweak the fabric slightly to get the joins to match up perfectly (known as easing). Sew with a straight stitch along the marked seam lines. Repeat for the other strips until all are joined. Press open all the seams, snipping away any loose threads as you go.

Now you know how to piece square patches, let's get on with some projects!

THE ONE-PATCH PILLOW

This very simple patchwork pillow is made up of four rows of six identical square patches (24 patches in total; finished size is 46 x 30 cm). Jazz it up with some appliqué lettering on the front, wooltastic tassels on the corners (see p. 46) or perhaps even work a beaded design on alternate squares .

You will need:
- Square template, 9 x 9 cm (includes seam allowance)
- Fabric for the patches
- Backing fabric, 47 x 31 cm (includes seam allowance)
- Tailor's chalk or pen
- Fabric scissors
- Sewing machine
- Matching thread
- Polyester stuffing

Making:
1. Use your template to mark and cut out 24 squares of fabric. Mark the 6mm seam allowances on the wrong side of each square. Lay your squares out on a flat surface in position, ready to piece.

2. Sew the squares into strips of six, using a straight stitch on the machine (p. 76).

3. Pin two strips together, matching up all the corners, and sew using a straight stitch. Repeat until all the strips are joined. Press out all the seams and snip away any loose threads.

4. Pin the patchwork piece to the backing fabric, right sides facing. Using a straight stitch on the machine, sew the edges with a 6 mm seam allowance, leaving an 8 cm gap in the middle of one side. Snip off all four corners close to the stitching and turn the pillow right side out, working out the corners into sharp points. Stuff the pillow, carefully working the stuffing into the corners. Fold over the hem at the gap and use a whipstitch (p. 61) to sew shut.

it's hip to be square

THE NINE-PATCH PILLOW

Now it's time to get some colour and pattern into the mix with this classic nine-patch project. This pillow is made of three rows of three 12.5 cm square patches (nine patches in total) and a 39 x 39 cm backing piece of fabric. Play around with prints and ditzy florals until you come up with the colour combinations that suit you best and use the instructions for the one-patch pillow (opposite) to make up.

THUNDERBIRD QUILT

I absolutely love beaded jewellery, so I was super excited when I discovered that my love for beading could easily be translated into patchwork – the principles for designing beading patterns are much the same as those for constructing geometric blocks of patchwork.

My favourite traditional beading motif is the lucky Thunderbird, and here it is in all its glory, relocated on a neon quilted blanket. The blanket is constructed with a patchwork front, plain back and a piece of wadding in the middle, which adds depth and warmth to the quilt. When using wadding, the three layers must always be stitched together, to keep them from moving. This is called quilting. Make sure you use thin wadding (or batting, as it is sometimes called) or you'll have trouble running the three layers through your machine.

You will need:

- Square template, 6.4 x 6.4 cm (includes 6 mm seam allowance)
- Scrap fabric for the patchwork front
- Plain backing fabric, 135 x 135 cm
- Fabric scissors
- Sewing machine
- Matching threads
- Tailor's chalk
- Wadding, 145 x 145 cm
- 555 cm (the sum of the edges of the quilt plus 15 cm extra) 6–8 cm double-fold binding tape

Making:

1. Make the front piece Use the colour chart opposite and the strip piecing technique described on p. 96 to construct the front of the quilt. Make sure you plan the design carefully before you start sewing – cut out all the squares (don't forget the seam allowance), then lay them out and build up the Thunderbird design on the floor, so you know exactly which squares to join together when. When strip piecing your squares, try to be as accurate as possible. Once your front piece has been constructed, carefully press all the seams out.

2. Make the 'quilt sandwich' Lay the backing fabric wrong side up on the floor. Lay the wadding on top, and then the patchwork front piece, right side up. Pin the three layers together carefully and tack using long running stitches. The wadding will be 5 cm longer on all sides, to allow for shrinkage during the quilting stage.

3. Quilt on the machine Following the grid made by your squares and working from the centre outwards, use a straight stitch on the machine (see p. 76) to stitch along every second or third seam line. This is called quilting in the ditch, and adds a little oomph without getting in the way of the design. Turn the quilt 90° and sew down every second or third seam line in this direction to make a quilted grid. Remove the tacking stitches and trim the edges.

4. Binding Pin the binding in place around the quilt, starting in the middle of one edge and mitring the corners as you go (see p. 68). Then using a topstitch (see p. 76), sew down close to the edge of the binding, making sure you stitch through all three layers. Stop stitching about 2.5 cm before the end of the binding, fold the raw edge under 1 cm and stitch to the end.

Say hello to your first quilt!

And I can guarantee it won't be your last, as there really is nothing more satisfying to create or beautiful to own than a homemade patchwork quilt. Why not design your own original quilt? Just get yourself some squared graph paper and make a design using geometric shapes to create words and patterns – the possibilities are endless!

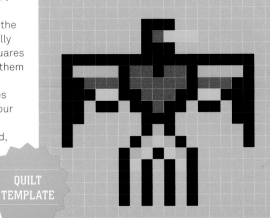

QUILT
TEMPLATE

GO GO
thunderbird
quilt

Front
441 x Square Patches - 2.5" x 2.5"
(with 1/4" seam allowance)
Template Size - 3" x 3"

305 x Pink squares
91 x Black squares
20 x Red squares
13 x Blue squares
12 x Yellow squares

Back
1 x large square - 52.5" x 52.5"
(with 1/4" seam allowance)
Template size - 53" x 53"

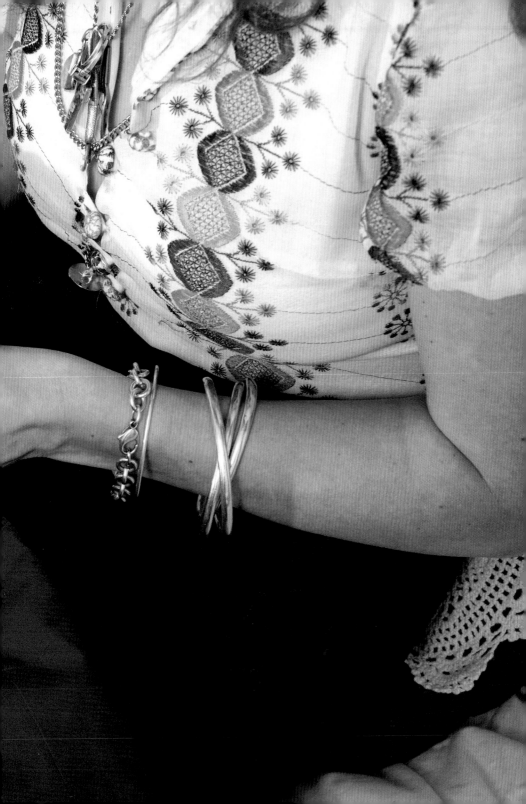

PART 2

KITCHE

BAKING · PRE

CRAFT

ERVING • KITCHEN
GARDENING

DELICIOUS BAKES
FOR EVERY OCCASION
Classic Victoria Sponge /
Cut & Come Again Cake /
Domino Petits Fours /
No-Need-to-Knead Bread /
Perfect Pastry /
Queen of Crafts Jam Tarts /
Sugar Cookies /
Broken-Heart Biscuits /
Button Biscuits /

BAKING

BAKING

Baking may be all the rage today but it wasn't that long ago that making cakes was something just your grandma did. Then everyone's favourite childhood sweetheart, the cupcake, came back into fashion, making headlines and taking the baking world by storm. Cake is cool again and the craze has spread thicker and faster than warm buttery icing, as cake is reinvented in all manner of new guises. So it seems this sugar high isn't set to crash and burn but a sweet-filled future is here to stay. And long may it reign supreme!

CAKES GONE BY

It all began with the first lady of cakes, Mrs Beeton. The original domestic diva and figurehead of Victorian housewifery, she brought baking to the masses with her hugely influential *Mrs Beeton's Book of Household Management*, a book so popular it's still in print to this day. If you haven't read it yet, I implore you to check it out – it's brilliant.

My mother (by her own admission) has never been a particularly enthusiastic cook. When it came to laying on a spread, she could always put things together with terrific style, but those things usually came from a fancy French patisserie. So when it came to experimenting in the kitchen as a kid, I was pretty much left to my own devices. I never had anyone standing over my shoulder telling me not to lick the spoon and I was given free rein to express myself through flour and sugar, often to great personal hilarity. One year, as a kid, on returning home from our annual family pilgrimage to Glastonbury music festival, I was inspired to make a cake in homage to the fun we had had, so I gathered together all my little pots of food colouring and mixed them together to create a great big muddy puddle of swirling colour – an early forerunner to my tie-dye icing technique (see p. 121).

Now I know I'm not the only one whose mother was less than interested in the art of baking. Many of our mothers (and perhaps even some of our grandmothers too) downed aprons to pursue work and other interests outside of the home. Hot on the heels of their feminist sisters, they were reluctant to be tied to the kitchen sink. And quite right too. But my great-grandmother was born into a very different era, a time when rationing meant people had to make the best use out of what little they had.

CAKE
IS
COOL

My granny remembers spending Saturday afternoons helping her mother bake up their meagre weekly butter and sugar ration into their once-a-week Saturday-night sweet treats.

While home baking is no longer a necessity, a growing awareness about the food we put in our bodies and a reluctance to rely on shop-bought alternatives has seen it make a major comeback. Especially after Nigella Lawson brought glamour to the art with her hugely popular TV series *How to Be a Domestic Goddess* and showed us all how wholesome and satisfying baking can be. And who can resist the smell of a home-baked cake? Happily, baking is no longer associated with outdated notions of female subservience but is now considered a prized skill, allowing you to indulge your creativity. So roll out the rolling pins – it's time to get stuck in and start your own baking bonanza!

EQUIPMENT

You'll probably have at least some of the necessary equipment in your kitchen kit already, and the stuff you don't yet have is best collected over time, as and when you need it.

CAKE TINS

An assortment of strong cake tins and pans in a variety of shapes and sizes will keep your baking interesting. Square, round, loaf, cupcake and novelty silicone moulds are all worthwhile investments. Make sure sponge tins are nice and deep (at least 4 cm) so your cakes have room to rise. Good-quality baking equipment tends to be expensive to buy new but it will last you a lifetime. Don't just look to department stores to source your tins and tools – keep your eyes peeled wherever you go. I once bought a brand-new Nordic Ware bundt tin for 50p from a car boot sale (they usually retail for £40); one man's trash really is another man's treasure.

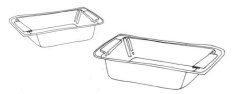

MIXING APPARATUS

A wooden spoon for mixing, a metal spoon for folding and a silicone spatula for almost everything else will be useful, and a small selection of mixing bowls in varying sizes.

SCALES

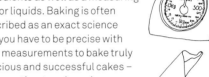

You will need a good pair of weighing scales for measuring out all your ingredients as well as a measuring jug for liquids. Baking is often described as an exact science and you have to be precise with your measurements to bake truly delicious and successful cakes – no guesstimates please!

ICING KIT

If you plan to dabble in the icing arts, an icing bag with several nozzle tubes will be indispensable for creating your own hand-drawn designs. Tala makes some deliciously retro reproduction icing tools, available from cookware shops or online. Most supermarkets stock a good selection of ready-to-go coloured icing tubes and writing pens, which are also nifty.

COOKIE CUTTERS

A selection of cookie cutters in various shapes and sizes will be useful for making biscuits and pretty pastries. I like to collect holiday-themed cutters as well as hearts, stars and letters – brilliant for baking biscuit messages. A set of fluted round cutters is also handy for making scones, small biscuits and mini tarts.

OTHER USEFUL TOOLS

A sieve for sifting flour and icing sugar, a rolling pin for rolling pastry, a wire rack for cooling biscuits and cakes, an electric beater for whisking eggs and a food mixer for whizzing up large batches of cakes quick smart can also be useful.

A pinch of this, a dash of that

Just a quick note on ingredients – obviously, using good-quality fresh ingredients will help you make a cake that is superior not only in taste but in texture and appearance too, so always try to buy the best you can afford. Particularly when it comes to bottles of flavourings and liquid essences: cheap ones have a nasty synthetic taste, the exact antithesis of what a home-baked cake should be. Caster sugar is best for baking sponge cakes, as its fine texture means it creams much better with butter than granulated sugar. Butter and eggs should always be used at room temperature to stop the cake batter from curdling when creamed. You can use butter or margarine for any of the recipes given below, but if you use butter, stick to the unsalted variety, which has a lighter (and obviously less savoury) taste better suited to cakes.

Check sell-by dates on spices, flours, raising agents and anything else that might have been lurking at the back of your cupboard for a while. Spices taste dreadful if they've been left to go stale, so always pop lids back on to pots when storing to ensure they keep their strong aromatic flavours for as long as possible. Always use a clean spoon when dipping between different pots of raising agents – they can easily become contaminated, which spoils their individual properties. And finally, if you want to keep weevils (annoying little flour beasties) at bay, store your baking flour in plastic Tupperware pots or boxes in a cool dry cupboard.

HOW TO MAKE A BETTER BATTER – BASIC BAKING KNOW-HOW

A bit of old-fashioned kitchen wisdom goes a long way when it comes to baking. I picked up most of what I know the hard way, by making just about every mistake in the book and going through countless cake catastrophes before I figured out cake-making right from cake-making wrong. If you want to bake like a pro, read on. ▶

PREHEATING THE OVEN
Preheating your oven to the right temperature is vital, so make sure you turn it on about 15 minutes before you need to use it. If your oven is temperamental, invest in an oven thermometer. Simply hang it or place it inside the oven, then as the oven heats up, check the temperature and adjust as necessary.

PREPARING YOUR TINS
Lining your tins will stop your cakes falling apart as you turn them out. Lining the base with a round of baking parchment is enough – use a pencil to draw around the bottom of your tin, then cut out. Grease both the bottom and the sides of the tin with butter or oil using a pastry brush or scrap of greaseproof paper, then place the paper waxy side down on to the bottom of your tin before pouring in your mixture. For a crispy sweet browned edge, grease the tins then dust with an equal mixture of flour and caster sugar, shake and tap out any surplus.

HALF BAKED?

Managing your oven temperatures and timings will make all the difference between a rock cake and a soft cake. But if you're not quite hip to your oven's quirks, how do you know when your cake is done? Test by removing the cake from the oven about 5–10 minutes before the suggested time and inserting a knife or a skewer into the centre of the cake. If it comes out completely clean, the cake is done. If it comes out with a cakey residue, cook it a little longer before testing again. Sponge cakes should be well-risen and golden brown but firm to the touch on both bottom and top. Biscuits and cookies should be checked almost by the minute – even the slightest overcooking can render them brittle. They are ready when they look evenly browned on top and feel crisp on the bottom.

COOLING

Always leave your cakes to cool for at least 5–10 minutes before turning out. Once you've carefully removed the cake from the tin, peel off the lining paper, then leave to cool completely on a wire rack before icing or storing. If you pack a cake away while still warm, it may become heavy in texture, so be patient.

STORING

Cakes are best eaten fresh; however, most will keep well for a few days in an airtight tin. Never store biscuits and cakes in the same container – the biscuits will absorb moisture from the cakes and lose their crispness. Plain biscuits can be stored stacked on top of one another but always remember to include a sheet of greaseproof paper between each layer. Iced or frosted biscuits and cookies should never be stacked up, as you will ruin any delicate decoration.

WHAT WENT WRONG?

When I first got serious about baking, back in the days of my Viva Cake midnight to morning bakeathons (see p. 126), this was a question that often used to trouble me. So many problems can arise doing what seems like such a simple task. But good baking, more than other cooking, is underpinned by science. A well-baked cake is a collection of well-executed techniques, timings and measurements. However, it is reassuring to know that for almost every mistake made, there is a logical explanation. And when it comes to baking, practice really does make perfect. Now, I know we haven't quite got anything in the oven just yet, but hang on to your mitts for a little longer and read through these common cake-wreck problems, to make sure your cake never falls flat on its face.

CAKE SANK

If the cake has sunk in the middle, it's most likely got something to do with the temperature of the oven. A sudden drop in temperature can be a common cause, so be vigilant about how and when you open the oven door once the cake is inside. Avoid opening it either too often or too suddenly and – the golden rule – don't even touch it for at least the first 15 minutes. Just avert your eyes completely. I know it can be all too tempting to take a sneaky peek – just don't do it!

CAKE TOO HEAVY

If your cake has a heavy, almost sticky texture, it has probably been baked at too high a temperature and for too short a time. I used to always get this wrong, trying to bake the cake quicker by whacking up the temperature dial – a sure-fire way to turn a tasty cake into a tasteless cake. So always cook your cakes according to the temperature and time given in the recipe, unless your oven has a particular quirk, in which case adjust it to suit (see 'Preheating the Oven', opposite).

CAKE TOO DRY

If your cake tastes dry and coarse, you have probably kept it too long in the oven. Cooking your cake slowly at a low temperature will cause it to dry out.

Oven Temperature Guide

GAS MARK	FAHRENHEIT	CELSIUS
¼	225	110
½	250	130
1	275	140
2	300	150
3	325	170
4	350	180
5	375	190
6	400	200
7	425	220
8	450	230
9	475	240

Handy Measures

Never try to mix different measuring systems when making a recipe – always stick to either metric or imperial. If you're anything like me and love American cookbooks, you are probably already familiar with cup measures. Again, don't be tempted to try and convert these; it will just get too tricky and you will only ever be able to find approximations. Instead, invest in a set of US cup measures.

Here are some handy guide measures to help you out:

1 tbsp = **3 tsp**
25 g/1 oz = **2 tbsp**
1 level tbsp = **15 ml**
1 level tsp = **5 ml**
25 g/1 oz flour = **1 heaped tbsp**
25 g/1 oz cocoa = **1 heaped tbsp**
25 g/1 oz sugar = **1 level tbsp**
25 g/1 oz butter or margarine = **2 level tbsp**

DELICIOUS BAKES FOR EVERY OCCASION

Okay, oven gloves and aprons at the ready – it's time to get your paws into the mix and start whipping up some seriously tasty treats that Mr Kipling himself would be proud of. If you're a beginner, start with the Victoria sponge recipe – to give it a twist, sandwich together with some fruity floral rose-petal jam (p. 140) and dust it in a delectable doily design (see p. 124). Or if you're already well practised in the baking arts, why not indulge your cakey creativity with some oh-so-adorable button biscuits (p. 119) or conjure up some edible glitter (see p. 125) to sprinkle like gold dust on to pimped-up pastries.

Tasty treat

CLASSIC VICTORIA SPONGE

I am definitely one for operating under the 'if it ain't broke then don't fix it' maxim. An oldie but a goodie, this classic recipe makes the most delicious fail-safe sponge. We've made these by the bucketload over the years, and to jazz things up a bit I like to add a touch of pink food colouring to the batter to mix a pretty-in-pink sponge that looks doubly gorgeous when piled with fresh juicy berries and hand-whipped cream. If you prefer to keep things classic, bake as normal and simply layer with jam (homemade, of course – see 'Preserving', p. 130) and dust generously with icing sugar.

YOU WILL NEED:

110 g (4 oz) self-raising flour
110 g (4 oz) unsalted butter or margarine
110 g (4 oz) caster sugar
2 eggs
1–2 tsp vanilla essence
2 x 15 cm sandwich tins

MAKING:

1. Preheat the oven to 180°C. In a medium-sized bowl, sift the flour twice to make the sponge really light and airy, then set aside.

2. In a large bowl, cream together the butter and sugar until light and fluffy. Beat in the eggs one at a time, then add the vanilla essence and mix well. Fold in the sifted flour.

3. Divide the batter between two well-greased and lined sandwich tins and bake for 20 minutes.

VARIATIONS

Chocolate sponge: sift 25 g (1 oz) of sieved cocoa with the flour.

Coffee sponge: add 2 tsp of instant coffee powder dissolved in 1 tbsp of hot water, and stir in after combining the eggs and vanilla.

Lemon sponge: add the grated rind and juice of half a lemon to the egg and vanilla mixture and stir.

CUT AND COME AGAIN CAKE

This is a dead-easy recipe for an all-in-one batch cake my grandma absolutely swears by. Brilliant if you want to make up a large quantity of sweet treats for a party (and see the domino petits fours, p. 114). The cut-and-come-again cake principle means there's always more then enough to go round. Spread the light fluffy sponge with a heavy layer of buttercream or drizzle with warm sugary icing and a rainbow of sprinkles.

YOU WILL NEED:

440 g (16 oz) sugar
350 ml (12 fl. oz) vegetable oil
4 eggs
425 g (15 oz) plain flour
2 tsp baking powder
2 tsp bicarbonate of soda
2 tsp vanilla essence
100 ml (4 fl. oz) milk
Round (23 cm) or square cake tin

MAKING:

NB If you have a food processor, you can simply whizz up all the ingredients in one go.

1. Preheat the oven to 180°C. In a large bowl, mix together the sugar and oil. Then beat in the eggs one at a time. Sift in the flour, baking powder and baking soda and mix until fully combined. Stir in the vanilla essence.

2. If the mixture is too thick, add some milk to make a looser batter. Then pour into a well-greased and lined tin.

3. Bake for 45 minutes or until the cake just begins to pull away from the sides of the tin.

VARIATIONS

Cherry-nut chocolate cake: add 50 g (2 oz) of sifted cocoa, 75 g (3 oz) of quartered fresh or glacé cherries and 50 g (2 oz) of chopped nuts.

Chocolate apple cake: omit the vanilla and milk and add 50 g (2 oz) of sifted cocoa along with 2 tsp of mixed spice and 225 ml (8 fl. oz) of stewed apple or apple sauce.

DOMINO PETITS FOURS

Cupcakes have been done to death but who can resist individual bite-sized cakes? These domino petits fours are the perfect alternative. Bake the cut-and-come-again cake recipe on p. 113 in an oblong or square tin. Once the cake has cooked and cooled completely, use a sharp knife to divide it into small rectangles. Then ice with either buttercream (see p. 122) or thick glacé icing (p. 121). If you are using buttercream, go wild and decorate with an assortment of sweets to create the domino effect: chocolate buttons, smarties or jazzies for the number spots and strawberry laces for the centre strips. If you are using glacé icing, ice while the cake is still in the tin, leave to set, then carefully turn out and cut into shapes with a sharp knife. Then use a chocolate glacé icing and a piping bag to ice the dots and strips.

It's a domino rally

NO-NEED-TO-KNEAD BREAD

Bread making can be a bit of a to-do, keeping your equipment warm, fussing about with yeast, then knuckle-knackering kneading often followed by disappointment when the bread fails to rise. That's why this method is such a winner; with no need to knead, it's the ultimate fuss-free recipe. You must keep all your utensils and bowls warm, so preheat the oven and rest them either to the side or on top of the oven as you start mixing your ingredients. Don't forget to grease and line your loaf tin – the lining should reach up over the sides of the tin, to make it easier for you to lift the bread at the end.

YOU WILL NEED:

450 g (1 lb) bread flour (I use a mix of half granary and half wholemeal, but you can use white or anything else you like)
1 tsp salt
2 tsp sugar
Seeds, seeds and more seeds (a teacupful or more of any seeds you fancy – flax, pumpkin, sunflower, poppy, sesame, caraway)
1 tsp dried yeast
1 tbsp vegetable oil
425 ml (¾ pint) warm water
Loaf tin

MAKING:

1. Preheat the oven to 200°C. In a large bowl, combine the flour, salt, sugar, seeds and yeast. Stir in the oil, then the water. Pour into your prepared loaf tin.

2. Rinse a clean cotton tea towel under a hot tap, wring out until damp, place on top of your loaf tin and leave the tin somewhere warm for 30 minutes (if enough heat is generated from the oven, sit it above or next to that, otherwise a warm dark cupboard will do). After 30 minutes, you will see that the dough has risen and is ready to be put into the oven. Now is the time to add a sprinkling of seeds.

3. Bake for 35–40 minutes. Remove the tin from the oven and turn it upside down on a clean surface for 10 minutes (I know this sounds strange, but trust me). Finally, turn the tin right side up and lift the bread out of the tin, remove the lining paper and leave on a wire rack to cool. Give it about 10–15 minutes before slicing up to eat.

the best thing since

THIS IS HOW I ROLL

HOW TO MAKE THE PERFECT PASTRY

When I make my own pastry, I feel like I deserve a medal, not because it's difficult but because so few people these days actually make the effort. But it's a great skill to have under your belt when you fancy knocking up something tasty for tea out of shop hours, and homemade pastry is so much more delicious.
Here are a few helpful hints:

Try to handle the dough as little as possible and keep all your equipment cold.

Keep the butter at room temperature to make mixing easier.

Incorporate air into the dough to keep the pastry light – use your fingertips to blend the ingredients, never the palms of your hands.

Add liquid gradually – too much water will create sticky unmanageable dough, and extra flour will cause it to become tough.

Use a hot oven to cook your pastry to keep it crisp and short.

KEEP
CALM
MAKE
JAM
TARTS

QUEEN OF CRAFTS JAM TARTS

These gloriously old-fashioned jam tarts are sure to give you a warm glow of nostalgia. Super simple to knock up, the fun comes in decorating them with mini pastry hearts and dusting down with vanilla-infused icing sugar (see p. 124).

YOU WILL NEED:

225 g (8 oz) plain flour
Pinch of salt
1 tbsp icing sugar, plus extra to dust
110 g (4 oz) butter or margarine
Cold water to mix
Red jam (see pp. 139–41 for recipes)
Caster sugar to dust
Rolling pin
Heart-shaped cookie cutter
Fluted round cutter
Cupcake tin

Makes about 18

MAKING:

1. Preheat the oven to 180°C. First make the pastry. In a large bowl, sieve together the flour, salt and 1 tbsp icing sugar. Add the butter or margarine and rub into the flour with your fingertips until it resembles breadcrumbs. Add cold water, 1 tbsp at a time, to bring the mixture into a dough. The dough is ready when it just about clings together. It shouldn't be sticky but should come cleanly off the bowl as you gather it together. Wrap the dough in some cling film or place in a polythene zip-lock bag and chill in the fridge for at least 30 minutes.

2. Once chilled, take the dough out of the fridge and leave to warm to room temperature. On a flat surface dusted with flour, roll the dough out about 0.5 cm thick. Cut rounds with a fluted pastry cutter just slightly larger than the holes of the cupcake tins – this will give some depth to the tarts. And don't forget to leave some pastry aside to make your heart-shaped decorations. Grease your tin and line each cupcake hole with a round of pastry, pressing down lightly with your fingers. Put a spoonful of jam in the centre of each round.

3. Using the leftover pastry, cut out some small hearts and place one on top of each tart. Glaze with some jam (using a pastry brush) and dust with caster sugar. Bake for 15 minutes or until light golden brown.

4. Remove from the oven, then dust each tart with icing sugar using a sieve and let cool on a wire rack. Watch your mouth on the jam – it can stay hot for some time, so try to be patient (I know it's hard) and let cool completely before tasting.

Queen of Craft jam tarts

BETTER BISCUITS

Homemade biscuits are a welcome addition to any elevenses or teatime. Here are a few tips to help you bake them at their best:

Always roll out your biscuit dough as evenly and thinly as possible.

Don't over-handle the dough as this will make it tough – try to get as many biscuits out of the first rolling as possible.

Always use sharp cookie cutters, and never twist the cutter.

Space your biscuits on greaseproof paper at least 5 cm apart. Brush the tops with milk (using a pastry brush) for a crispy browned edge.

Allow your biscuits and cookies to cool completely on wire racks before icing or storing.

Store biscuits in an airtight tin as soon as they have cooled. If they are left out too long, they will absorb moisture from the air and become soft.

SUGAR COOKIES

A good sugar cookie should taste buttery with a lingering hint of vanilla. Here's a deliciously sweet version of this year-round favourite. Decorate your biscuits with icing, frosting, sprinkles or sweeties, bake them for holidays, gifts or with special messages for parties and events.

YOU WILL NEED:

110 g (4 oz) butter or margarine
150 g (5 oz) sugar
225 g (8 oz) plain flour
1 tsp baking powder
1 egg
1 tsp vanilla essence
Rolling pin
Cookie cutters
Baking sheet

MAKING:

1. Preheat the oven to 180°C. In a bowl, cream the butter and sugar until light and fluffy. In a separate bowl, sift the flour and baking powder together.

2. Gradually add the beaten egg into the butter and sugar mixture, mix well, then stir in the vanilla essence.

3. Add the flour mixture to the wet ingredients to form a dough. If it looks a bit soft, add some more flour; if it gets too thick, add a drop or two of milk. Cover the dough with cling film and leave in the fridge for 30 minutes.

4. Remove from the fridge, dispose of the cling film and on a flat surface dusted with flour, roll the dough out to about 0.5 cm thick. Cut out your desired shapes and place on to baking sheets covered in greaseproof paper. Bake for 10–15 minutes or until golden brown. Leave to cool completely on wire racks before icing.

NB To make a chocolate version, add 25 g (1 oz) cocoa powder to the sifted flour mixture.

BROKEN HEART BISCUITS

Make some broken heart biscuits to be served with a side order of heartache or for the ultimate anti-Valentine's Day treat. Bake cookies as above in a selection of heart shapes. Then make up some thick red or pink glacé icing (see p. 121). With a piping bag or a small spoon, ice a zigzag down the centre of the heart. Then leave one half of the cookie plain and fill the other half in with icing. Finish with a sprinkle of hundreds and thousands and leave to set.

BUTTON BISCUITS

Make some adorable button biscuits to bring to your next sewing meet. Divide the dough and tint it with different shades of food colouring (go easy here – lurid colours ruin the effect) by kneading each colour into a batch of dough. Roll out as above, then use small round cutters to cut out discs of dough. Lightly press another cutter, about 3 mm smaller, against the disc to make an indented line around the edge. Make the buttonholes with a cocktail stick or skewer. Then lay on to baking sheets lined with greaseproof paper, dust with granulated sugar and bake until the edges just start to brown.

broken heart biscuits

button biscuits

WHIP IT GOOD! ICING FOR ALL OCCASIONS

Adding a few simple icing recipes and techniques to your baking repertoire means you'll always have an iced gem to be proud of. It's surprising what even the simplest decorations can do. A few things to keep in mind before you start:

Never attempt to ice a cake before it has cooled completely – the icing won't stick and will most likely melt off in a big splodge.

Try to keep the surface of the cake as level as possible for icing. If the top has risen up into a peak or a dome, which often happens with sponge cakes, just level off with a sharp serrated knife.

Always remove excess loose crumbs before icing by brushing the cake down with a pastry brush.

Make Your Own Icing Bag

Icing bags are cheap and easy to get hold of but just in case you get caught short, here's a simple way to make your own:

1. Cut out a 25 cm square of greaseproof paper and fold it in half diagonally.

2. Work the triangle into a cone shape by overlapping two of the edges until the bottom of the cone has a sharp point. Fold the point in at an angle.

3. To use, fill the bag with icing (be careful not to overfill), fold over the top of the bag and press the icing down towards the point. Finally, snip off the point ready to ice.

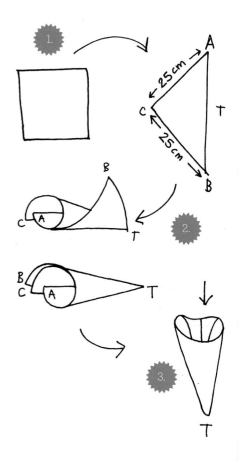

★★★ Glacé Icing ★★★

A well-loved classic, glacé icing can be made to suit almost any flavour or consistency of cake or biscuit. Keep a bag of icing sugar in the back of your cupboard at all times so you can whip up some tasty icing at a moment's notice. All you have to do is sift some icing sugar into a bowl, add a touch of warm water (a little at a time), plus any flavourings and/or colourings (see below), and mix with a wooden spoon until the icing reaches the desired consistency.

Remember: For most cakes and biscuits, mix the icing to a thick pouring consistency, adding only a scant tsp of water at a time (alongside flavourings and/or colourings to suit the occasion).

Always use at once. If using on a cake, pour the icing on and gently spread it to reach the sides with a dry palette knife or spoon. You can bring the icing to the edge by turning the cake. Try to avoid spreading it around the surface too much, as this will create an uneven set. Arrange your decorations while the icing is still soft and leave to dry before moving, to prevent the icing from cracking and wrinkling.

MIX IT UP
Here are some different flavour and colour combinations to try:

Almond – Mix icing sugar with almond essence and water. Tint with pink food colouring.

Lemon – Mix icing sugar with freshly squeezed lemon juice. Tint with yellow food colouring.

Vanilla – Mix icing sugar with vanilla essence and water. Tint with pink or yellow food colouring.

Coffee – Mix icing sugar with a spoonful of instant coffee or coffee essence and some water to melt.

Chocolate – Mix icing sugar with either 1 tbsp cocoa powder or some melted chocolate.

★★★ Glacé Icing Effects ★★★

Now you have your glacé icing, with a little know-how you can create some simple yet stunning effects to give your cakes (or cookies) that professional edge.

Covering Edges
Spread the glacé icing along the sides of the cake. With both hands firmly holding the cake by the base and top, roll the sides in a tray lined with a layer of greaseproof paper and either chopped nuts, hundreds and thousands, desiccated coconut, grated chocolate or biscuit crumbs.

Spider's Web
Ice the top of your cake with some thick white glacé icing. Then, with a contrasting coloured icing, pipe a set of rings an equal distance apart, moving from the centre of the cake out towards the edge. With a skewer or toothpick, draw a set of lines from the edge of the cake to the centre, and then draw an equal number of lines in the opposite direction, from the centre of the cake to the edge.

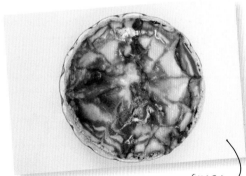

crazy tie-dye cake

Tie-Dye
Now add some colour imitating the effect of tie-dye (check out how to tie-dye your threads for real on p. 213). Ice the cake with a bright base colour. Then choose another two contrasting colours and mix up in separate bowls. With each contrasting colour, ice a set of rings from the centre of the cake out towards the edge. Then use a skewer or toothpick to draw a set of lines from the edge of the cake to the centre, and repeat in the opposite direction, from the centre of the cake to the edge.

★★★ *Buttercream Icing* ★★★

Another simple yet delicious icing you can use to both ice and fill your cakes is buttercream – butter and icing sugar are creamed together to a thick spreadable consistency. If the mixture is a little stiff, add a drop or two of milk to make it easier to spread on to the cake. To make really good buttercream icing, you must cream the butter and sugar together properly – taking short cuts like melting or warming the butter first will only make an oily icing, so don't do it! Ideally, the butter should be at room temperature before you use it.

YOU WILL NEED:
50 g (2 oz) butter or margarine
110 g (4 oz) icing sugar
2 tsp vanilla essence

MAKING:
1. In a bowl, beat the butter with a fork until pale and creamy.

2. Gradually add in the sugar and continue to cream.

3. Add a drop or two of milk along with the essence and beat till smooth and creamy.

──────── VARIATIONS ────────

Chocolate: replace the vanilla essence with 1 tbsp of sifted cocoa powder.

Peppermint: replace the vanilla essence with 1 tsp peppermint essence and a scant drop of green food colouring – keep it pale!

★★★ *Pipe Dreams* ★★★

Ever wondered how to get those professional swirls and spirals on top of your cupcakes? Well, here's how it's done. Practice makes perfect but once you get into the groove, you'll have this trick down so quick you'll wonder how you ever got by without it. You will need a cupcake and a piping bag filled with buttercream with a star-shaped nozzle tip. Hold the icing bag in a vertical position hovering just above the surface of the cake. Then . . .

Pipe a swirl – Squeeze the icing bag and press down towards the tip, working from the centre of the cake towards the outer edge in one long continuous circular movement, then remove the pressure and pull the tip away.

Pipe a spiral – Squeeze the icing bag and press down towards the tip, working in the opposite direction this time, from the outer edge in towards the centre, in one long continuous circular movement, then remove the pressure and pull the tip away. Then pipe another swirl on top of the first, not as wide or as large, working from the edge again and pulling up from the centre to finish.

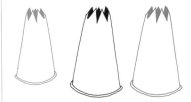

OH-SO-SIMPLE DECORATIONS

Here are some tried-and-tested techniques for when time is short but you're still keen to impress:

Brush the cake with some melted honey, golden syrup or apricot jam (see p. 139 for recipe), place a paper doily on top and dust with icing sugar. Carefully lift off the doily to reveal the sugar pattern beneath.

Ice a cake with some glacé or buttercream icing, then decorate with well-positioned jelly sweets, silver dragee balls, chocolate buttons, sugar flowers or anything else you fancy. A word of advice: decide what effect you want to create before you ice.

Make an iced snow cake with some coloured desiccated coconut. In a bowl, rub two or three drops of food colouring into the coconut with your fingers until mixed. Then sprinkle like a snowstorm on to a cake covered in thick white creamy icing.

Make your own edible glitter or coloured sugars (see p. 125) to dust down beautifully piped buttercream spirals and swirls (see p. 122).

INFUSED SUGARS

Infused sugars carry the rich scents and flavours of aromatic spices. They can be used instead of regular sugar: added to fresh fruit and cereals for breakfast, with your tea and coffee (vanilla sugar on top of a hot frothy latte is divine) or in your baking, either added to the batter or as delightful dusty toppings. Best of all, they make seriously sweet gifts to give to friends and family in place of traditional jams and chutneys. I like to make up cheerful labels and then tie down with doilies and ribbons (see p. 149 for more tips on prettying up jars).

YOU WILL NEED:
1 airtight jar
(Kilner jars are ideal)
1 packet of sugar
(granulated, caster or icing)
1–2 vanilla pods or
cinnamon sticks
or 2 tbsp dried lavender buds

MAKING:
1. Fill the jar halfway with sugar. Cut the vanilla pods or the cinnamon sticks into 1 cm pieces and place in the jar. If using lavender, sprinkle the buds into the sugar and shake to distribute. Add in the rest of the sugar or until the jar is full.

2. Close the container and store in a cool dark cupboard for 3 weeks to allow the scent and flavour to infuse the sugar. Give the sugar a shake every few days to get the aromas circulating. If using lavender, sift it out and refill the jar with the sugar.

Coloured Sugar

Place a small amount of sugar in a bowl, then add two or three drops of food colouring and work in with your fingers until the sugar is evenly covered. Leave to dry before storing in an airtight container. Use as dainty decoration for biscuits and cakes.

EDIBLE GLITTER

Edible glitter is a heavenly creation – a sweet sugary fairy dust that can be used to add a touch of glitz to frosted cakes and iced biscuits. And it's really quite simple to make yourself at home. Kept dry in an airtight container, it will last for months. Gum arabic is a natural food stabilizer available in the baking aisle of most big supermarkets.

YOU WILL NEED:
2 tbsp gum arabic
2 tbsp hot water
Food colouring (optional)

MAKING:
1. Place the gum arabic and the water in a bowl over a saucepan of simmering water and stir until the gum is completely dissolved. If you want to colour the glitter, do so now with some food colouring. (Uncoloured glitter will appear silver. A mixture of yellow and orange will come out gold.)

2. Have ready a deep glass bowl. Use a pastry brush (must be 100% clean!) to evenly coat the surface of the bowl with the gum mixture. Try to cover as much surface area as possible.

3. Leave to set in a warm dry room for at least 12 hours. The mixture will have formed a thin film against the glass. Remove the gum with a sharp knife and scrape off into another bowl. To make smaller flakes, break up with a rolling pin or sift through a strainer.

FONDANT CANDY DECORATIONS

Use this easy-cook no-boil fondant candy to make 3D decorations using silicone moulds or roll out like dough and cut out with cookie cutters to make flat shapes. Always colour delicately and don't overdo it with the flavouring – any more than a hint will be sickly sweet. Fondant candy can also be dipped or rolled in melted chocolate for a decadent touch. Add a sprinkle of crushed candy cane at Christmas for some festive cheer or some popping candy for a bit of rockin' fun.

YOU WILL NEED:
50 g (2 oz) butter or margarine
110 g (4 oz) condensed milk
450 g (1 lb) icing sugar, sifted
2 tsp flavouring
1 tsp food colouring
Rolling pin
Cookie cutters or moulds

MAKING:
1. In a large bowl, cream the butter. Then gradually mix in the condensed milk. Slowly sift in the icing sugar and continue to mix. Add flavouring and colour if desired (always very gradually). Knead the mixture with your hands to form a dough.

2. Either pack the candy into moulds and leave in the fridge for 3 hours before using. Or roll out on to a clean surface lightly dusted with icing sugar and use mini cookie cutters to cut out before chilling. Store wrapped in cling film or foil.

Fun with Flavourings

Vanilla – Mix with vanilla essence and yellow or pink food colouring.

Peppermint – Mix with peppermint essence and green food colouring.

Almond – Mix with almond essence and yellow or pink food colouring.

Lemon – Mix with lemon essence and yellow food colouring.

Rose – Mix with ½ tsp of rose water essence and pink food colouring.

Orange – Mix with orange flower water and orange food colouring.

CAUTION: Never pack peppermint-flavoured treats alongside other flavoured sweets and candies – as the scent is so strong it will affect the taste of anything else it comes into contact with.

CAKE BAKERS UNITE

Back in 2004, my friends and I organized a monthly club night called Viva Cake – it was a rock'n'roll tea dance that celebrated a bygone age and we served up teas and home-baked cakes on vintage crockery and antique linens.

To keep our guests entertained, we had dance lessons, bingo sessions, tarot card readings, arm wrestling tournaments and, most importantly, a cake competition. Now you have your baking ammo loaded and ready to go, you might want to think about holding a friendly bake-off with some fellow enthusiasts – fun for parties, club nights, fundraisers and any other get-togethers. Here are some tips on how to do it properly:

BAKE OFF!

GET YOUR CAKES HERE

Advertise your bake-off with a flier, invite or a round-robin email explaining the rules and how it works (and be clear about what entries you will accept – cakes, cupcakes, biscuits or all three).

Put together your prizes. Handmade cake-related paraphernalia is always good – try cake pincushions (p. 70) or rosettes (see opposite).

On the day, arrange a table display somewhere in view but out of the way of the other festivities (to ensure no accidents happen – especially if alcohol is on the agenda). Don't forget to add a name marker next to each cake.

Gather a panel of judges together to pick a clear first, second and third before presenting the prizes.

We always used to hand out homemade rosettes for first, second and third prizes – they add a homespun and thoughtful touch.

YOU WILL NEED:

Cardboard
(old greetings cards or
a cereal box would be ideal)
Scrap fabric
Scrap felt
Long lengths of 2
different widths of ribbon
Safety pins
Scissors
Needle and matching threads
Sewing machine (optional)

MAKING:

1. Cut out a cardboard circle to make the base of the rosette head. For a regular-sized rosette, the circle should be 5–8 cm in diameter. Cut out a circle of fabric twice the diameter of the card.

2. Cut out a felt number 1, 2 or 3. Pin it in place in the centre of the fabric and stitch down using either a whipstitch (p. 61) or a decorative blanket stitch (see p. 62).

3. Centre the cardboard circle behind the fabric front and with a knotted thread make a running stitch (see p. 61) around the edge of the fabric. Carefully pull the stitches into a gather (with the cardboard circle enclosed) and secure with a few firm fix stitches to the back (see p. 62).

4. To make the frill to sit around the circle, cut a long strip of fabric about 8 cm wide and sew a running stitch around the edge of the strip. Gently pull the thread to gather in the fabric, forming a ruche. Then sew this in place around the cardboard base.

5. Sew the thin ribbon on top of the wider ribbon strip down the centre. Then gather and fold the ribbon strips into pleats, securing with a few fix stitches. Trim the bottoms into a V, then attach to the back of the cardboard head with a few stitches.

6. Cut out another piece of felt to cover the back of the cardboard. Sew a safety pin to the centre of the felt, then attach to the back of the cardboard with a whipstitch to give a neat finish.

Winner

PRESERVING

BLUEBERRY

CHERRY

STRAWBERRY

ROSE WATER &

RASPBERRY

STRAW-BERRY

Blackberry & Apple

RHUBARB & GINGER

BLACKBERRY *Damson*

APPLE GINGER

MULLED PLUM APRICOT

PRESERVING

JAM MAKING HAS MADE A COMEBACK! The back-to-basics food movement of recent years is inspiring a new generation of jam makers to preserve their cooking heritage. Despite being one of the oldest kitchen skills, home preserving also chimes with the seasonal-cooking zeitgeist in making the best and economical use of yummy fresh produce. And nothing tastes sweeter than a gorgeous glut of your own delicious homemade jam, marmalade or chutney.

For those not yet in the know, the idea of making your own may still conjure up thoughts of dreary domestic toil and trouble. One of the most common misconceptions about preserving is that you have to cook up huge quantities of the sticky stuff, sweating over a hot stove like a kitchen wench. Not true – in actual fact, jam making couldn't be simpler. It takes very little effort, hardly any specialist equipment, only a handful of ingredients and is always best made up in small batches, which take less time to boil and reach a good set. So once you get the basic principles of preserving down, you'll see that making your own jams, marmalades and chutneys is not only good fun but also a tasty way to add a bit of zing and sweet sparkle to your homemade tarts and cakes (see recipes on pp. 113 and 117). Or better yet, try it on hot buttered toast for breakfast or smeared on to freshly baked bread for tea (see p. 114 for a perfect no-knead recipe). What's more, home preserves make the most delicious edible gifts – what could be better than sharing the bountiful fruits of your labour with friends and family? But be warned: once you (and they) have discovered the first-class freshness and flavour of homemade jam, it will be difficult to go back to eating the shop-bought variety, even the ones with fancy French labels. **Now start spreading the word!**

Loves Me, Loves Me Not
ROSE PETAL JAM

SPREAD
the
LOVE

PRESERVING TRADITION

As a self-confessed champion of the WI, I am fascinated by its long and well-documented history of voluntary food production. The huge contribution WI members made to fruit preservation schemes at the height of wartime rationing earned them the now infamous tag 'Jam and Jerusalem'. Generally used today to dismiss the WI's activities as just hymn singing and jam making, it actually refers to their wartime efforts to help feed an undernourished nation and prevent mass food wastage. 'Jerusalem', a socialist protest song, became the WI's unofficial anthem – how radical can you get? The Shoreditch Sisters have joined this time-honoured tradition – we have been known to whip up jam for the masses. Using your skills to produce jars of jewel-like jelly and marvellous marmalade to sell at local fundraisers and fêtes is a fun and charitable way to spread seasonal cheer.

EQUIPMENT

Most of the equipment needed for jam making is more than likely already part of your standard kitchen kit, so with the addition of one or two added extras you will be all set.

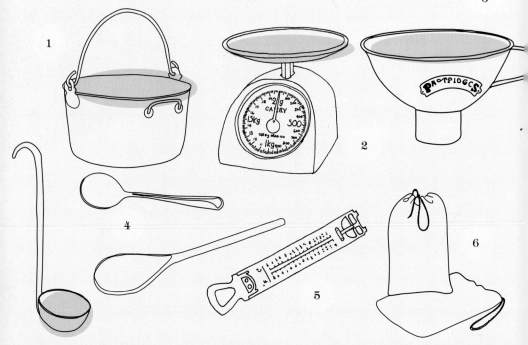

1. PRESERVING PAN
A large heavy-based stainless steel pan is essential for cooking any kind of preserve. A tall straight-sided metal pan will do, but the more traditional jam 'maslin' pans, wider at the top, should last you a lifetime if you decide to invest. Whichever you choose, it should at least have a thick base, to spread the heat during cooking and prevent the jam from burning during rapid boiling. It should also be tall enough to be only half full when all the ingredients have been added, so the jam won't froth over the edge. Always simmer and boil the fruit without a lid.

2. SCALES
To weigh out the fruit and sugar, you'll need a good pair of kitchen scales.

3. JAM FUNNEL
Another essential, as there really is nothing more irritating than covering both yourself and your kitchen with hot sticky jam while filling jars. Buy a stainless steel funnel made especially for jam making if you can – most good kitchen shops and department stores sell them. Failing that, a standard plastic funnel will do for smaller-cut jams and marmalades.

4. SPOONS
Long-handled wooden and metal spoons are useful for stirring, but you'll also need a latticed skimming ladle or spoon for removing the fruit scum at the end of the boiling process.

5. SUGAR THERMOMETER
Definitely not an essential – I have made pots and pots in the past without one, preferring to use my instinct and the good old-fashioned saucer test (see p. 137) for checking setting point. However, if you do happen to have one, it can be useful for measuring the correct setting temperature: 105–110°C (220–230°F).

6. MUSLIN BAGS
Buy them in packs from kitchen shops or homeware stores like Robert Dyas, and use to infuse spices, herbs and other heavenly flavourings in your preserves. Use them too to tie up pips, kernels, fruit skin and pith, which can then be conveniently removed and disposed of before boiling. The bags themselves can be reused – just wash them out and hang to dry before storing away for your next jam session.

7. JAM COVERS
You will need cellophane circles, wax-paper discs and rubber bands for covering and sealing the preserves, all of which you can buy ready-made in kits from a supermarket, kitchen shop or homeware store. These are absolutely essential for preventing mould and bacteria from forming on the surface of the preserves during storage.

8. JARS
Make a habit of collecting and reusing glass jars. Ask your friends and family to collect them for you too. I pick up monthly stockpiles from my nearest and dearest, so I've an epic assortment that get well-used and merry-go-round all my kitchen creations. Always check for chips, cracks and other blemishes and never use damaged jars or lids.

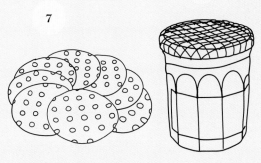

7

8

REMEMBER: ALL YOUR EQUIPMENT MUST BE THOROUGHLY CLEANED, AND YOUR JAM JARS STERILIZED (SEE P. 134) TO PREVENT BACTERIA OR MOULD FORMING ON THE SURFACE OF THE PRESERVE. I DON'T NEED TO TELL YOU THAT MOULD PLUS JAM IS NOT A GOOD COMBINATION . . .

HOW TO STERILIZE JARS

Residue food and dirt will spoil fresh jam
so it's really important to sterilize your jars.
Here's how you do it:

1. Remove any old labels and clean in a
dishwasher or by soaking in hot soapy water.
Dry thoroughly with a tea towel.

2. Half an hour or so before you are ready to fill
the jars, place both the jar and the lid upside
down on a baking tray and put in a cool oven
(140°C) for 15 minutes.

3. Remove the jars from the oven (being very
careful not to burn yourself!) and fill
immediately while the jars are still hot.

STORING YOUR JAMS

Unopened correctly sealed homemade jams
and preserves can be kept for up to a year.
For best results store in a cool dark cupboard
and once opened always keep in the fridge.

Okay, so let's break it down: all you really need to make jam or marmalade is fruit, sugar and pectin – it's as simple as that. Jam is essentially boiled fruit pulp and sugar, and to reach a successful setting point it must contain the correct ratio of sugar, fruit acid and pectin – getting this right is the key to obtaining the perfect preserve.

PECTIN

Pectin is a natural gelling agent found in the skin, pith and pips of fruit and vegetables and is essential to making a well-set jam or marmalade. Traditionally, most recipes call for the addition of lemon juice to give an added pectin kick but I prefer to use liquid apple pectin. Certo is the brand I go for, which can be found in the baking aisle of most good supermarkets. Usually, 1–2 tbsp in each batch is plenty to obtain a good set.

FRUIT

You will often need large quantities of fruit, so when choosing, keep it seasonal if you can – it will be kinder on your purse. Visit markets to get inspired by what's on offer. I once went shopping for plums, hoping to make a mulled Christmas jam, and came home with damsons, after which a whole new world of previously undiscovered fruit blossomed before me – yum!

Always make sure you use the freshest fruit possible, preferably in peak condition or even slightly under-ripe. Never, ever use over-ripe or damaged fruit as not only will it have a much lower pectin content (and so mess up your fruit-to-pectin ratio) but it could also impair the overall flavour of your jam.

▼ ▼ ▼ ▼ ▼ ▼ ▼ ▼ ▼ ▼ ▼ ▼ ▼

PECTIN RICH?

All fruits naturally contain varying levels of sugar, pectin and acid.

HIGH-PECTIN FRUIT – Citrus fruits, apples, plums, damsons, gooseberries, blackcurrants, redcurrants, cranberries.

MEDIUM-PECTIN FRUIT – Apricots, raspberries, greengages, elderberries, blackberries.

LOW-PECTIN FRUIT – Strawberries, cherries, pears, rhubarb, figs, grapes, peaches, blueberries.

SUGAR

White granulated sugar is best for jam making, although you can buy special jam and preserving sugars with added pectin from the supermarket, which are perfect for using with lower-grade pectin fruits to guarantee a good set. Most recipes use a classic half-and-half proportion of fruit to sugar, and unless a recipe calls for something different, it's best to stick to this tried-and-tested ratio.

CHERRY
BOMB
JAM !!

WE BE
★ jamming ★

KICK OUT THE JAMS

So now you have all your basic kit ready, including jam pan, jars, lids and covers, it's time to make like those famous Detroit rockers MC5 and get ready to 'kick out the jams'. Why not gather some friends together for a jamming session? Just pick a recipe from the following pages, and let's begin…

1. COOKING THE FRUIT Before you begin, make sure all your fruit has been washed and drained dry. Then prepare it by removing stalks, pith, skin and stones, taking out pips or cores, removing berry tops and chopping everything into small bite-sized pieces. Put your prepared fruit in the pan, and, if the recipe calls for it, add water or spices now, and any pips or stones tied up into muslin bags, which will steep in the cooking fruit. Simmer slowly on a low heat (don't let the mixture boil) until the skins of the fruit have softened and the pieces have broken down to a mushy pulp. How long this takes will depend largely on the kind of fruit you are using, but it should be between 15 and 60 minutes. Hard-skinned fruit, like apples, will take longer than soft-skinned fruit and berries, especially with added water (which should be reduced by at least a third before you move on to the next stage). If you're using them, muslin bags should now be removed and any excess juice squeezed back into the pan.

2. ADDING THE SUGAR Once the fruit has cooked, add the sugar and liquid pectin and stir constantly until dissolved. Do not begin to boil until you are sure that all of the sugar is properly dissolved, as this will lead to the jam crystallizing.

3. BOILING THE FRUIT Finally, bring the jam to a rapid rolling boil until it reaches setting point. Only stir occasionally now – and be careful as the jam can get very hot and might spit. The boiling process can take anything from 10 to 40 minutes, according to the type of preserve and the quantity you are making. So keep testing the jam at regular intervals, using either a sugar thermometer – setting point is at 105–110°C (220–230°F) – or my preferred method, the saucer test (see box, below).

4. FINISHING THE JAM Check to see whether it needs skimming. Again, this depends on the kind of fruit you use – some will produce more surface scum than others (strawberries are particularly frothy and need considerable skimming with a latticed spoon or ladle). If your recipe calls for the addition of a flavouring or liqueur, add it now as the jam is cooling off, taking care as the jam may bubble and spit.

5. FILLING AND COVERING THE JARS Stir gently to distribute the fruit and then funnel the jam into hot, sterilized jars. Seal immediately with a wax-paper disc placed wax side down on to the jam, making sure you don't trap any air bubbles. Finally, place a cellophane circle on top of the jar and secure in place with a rubber band before closing with your lid. Use a hot damp cloth to wipe any excess jam that may have escaped during the filling process. Leave to cool before labelling (see p. 149 for how to make your own) and tying down with a decorative cover and ribbon.

★ ★ ★

THE SAUCER TEST – TESTING JAM FOR SETTING POINT

Chill a small saucer in the fridge. Remove the jam from the heat, then drop a teaspoonful of jam on to the cold saucer and put back into the fridge for 2 minutes. If the jam seems to have the right texture and consistency after cooling on the plate, and wrinkles when pushed with a spoon or a finger, it is set. If the jam is not yet ready, return to the heat and boil for a little longer and try again.

Now put your skills and your taste buds to the test! Get your friends round for a tea party with your oh-so-luscious cakes (see p. 113 for some recipes) and lovely homemade jam. They'll soon be begging for tips from the new Queen of Jams.

THIS IS JAM HOT

STICKY JAM RECIPES

SUGAR AND SPICE APPLE AND GINGER JAM

This spicy fruity jam is a sure-fire winner – the subtle but sharp ginger bites back against the sweet apple. Use cooking apples if you can, as they have a higher pectin content than eating apples.

1.4 kg (3 lbs) cooking apples
50 g (2 oz) fresh ginger,
grated or finely chopped
1 cinnamon stick
Water to cover
1.4 kg (3 lbs) sugar
1 tbsp liquid pectin

Peel and core the apples and cut into quarters. Place the peel, core, pips and chopped ginger in a muslin bag and put in the pan with the chopped apples and the cinnamon stick. Add just enough water to cover the fruit and simmer until tender. Remove the cinnamon stick and muslin bag, squeezing any excess juice back into the pan. Add the sugar and liquid pectin and stir until dissolved. Bring to a rapid rolling boil and cook until setting point is reached. Remove from the heat, skim off any scum and then stir to distribute fruit before funnelling into hot sterilized jars. Seal and cover.

BLACKBERRY BLAST JAM

This rich berry jam reminds me of late summer days spent foraging in overgrown hedgerows as a kid. The burst-in-your-mouth flavour of blackberry is wonderful both on its own and when combined with other fruits, like apples or pears. The perfect accompaniment to pastries and tarts.

1.4 kg (3 lbs) blackberries
Water to cover
1.4 kg (3 lbs) sugar
2 tbsp liquid pectin

Prepare as for Apple and Ginger Jam above. Simmer the berries until they are tender, then crush with a spoon for a smoother set, if preferred.

CHERRY BOMB JAM

Bittersweet cherry jam can be made with dark cherries, sour cherries, morellos or whatever happens to be in season. Add a shot of fruit liqueur or a hit of cherry brandy for a more intense flavour. This crimson jam will taste darkly delicious spooned on to cakes, sandwiched in between biscuits or on a batch of jam tarts (see recipe on p. 117).

1.4 kg (3 lbs) cherries, stoned
Water to cover
1.4 kg (3 lbs) sugar
2 tbsp liquid pectin
3 tbsp cherry brandy (optional)

Prepare as for Apple and Ginger Jam above. The cherry stones should be put in the pan with the fruit and water, in a muslin bag. Add the cherry brandy after skimming, if using.

AWESOME APRICOT JAM

Nothing has that fresh fruity tang like a pot of homemade apricot jam and happily apricots are bountiful and relatively inexpensive in season. Try cracking a couple of the apricot kernels into the mix to add a subtle hint of bitter almond. Apricot jam can also be used in your home baking as a glaze –it gives a light glossy sheen to cakes and helps with sticking down decorations. Try out my doily icing trick on p. 124.

1.4 kg (3 lbs) fresh apricots,
halved and stoned
Water to cover
1.4 kg (3 lbs) sugar
1 tbsp liquid pectin

Prepare as for Apple and Ginger Jam above. Crack the apricot stones open, remove the kernels and blanch them in boiling water to remove the brown skins. Then drop a white kernel into each jar before filling with jam.

DAZZLIN' DAMSON JAM

Classier cousin of our standard plum, damsons are tougher skinned and more acidic and make the perfect preserving fruit. As they are simmered, they become sweet and almost spicy in flavour and turn a rich shade of deep purple.

1.4 kg (3 lbs) damsons,
stoned and quartered
1 cinnamon stick (optional)
Water to cover
1.4 kg (3 lbs) sugar
1 tbsp liquid pectin

The stones cling to the fruit and can be tricky to remove, so if it gets too fiddly, simply let them be and just remember to remove them before the rapid boil with a latticed spoon. Prepare as for Apple and Ginger Jam (p. 139). Place the stones in a muslin bag and put in the pan with the fruit and water.

BE-BOPPIN' BERRY STRAWBERRY JAM

This classic recipe calls for considerably less sugar than the usual ratio as strawberries can become unpleasantly sweet during the preserving process, often leaving very little of the original fruit flavour. Bring some summer sunshine to your breakfast table and spread this jam on toast, or tart it up for tea on a soft and fluffy Victoria sponge (see p. 113).

1.4 kg (3 lbs) strawberries,
tops removed and halved
900 g (2 lbs) sugar
2 tbsp liquid pectin

Prepare as for Apple and Ginger Jam (p. 139). Simmer the berries until tender, then crush with a spoon for a smoother set, if preferred.

LOVES ME, LOVES ME NOT ROSE-PETAL JAM

This fruit and floral combination makes a lightly perfumed jam, reminiscent of exotic Turkish delight. Add as much or as little rose water as suits your personal taste. If you're feeling adventurous, use layered up in a traditional Victoria sponge (see p. 113) for a decadent teatime treat. This delicious and unusual jam also makes a super-cute Valentine's Day gift, so whip up some heart-shaped labels and get fancy with your ribbons.

1.4 kg (3 lbs) strawberries,
tops removed and halved
900 g (2 lbs) sugar
2 tbsp liquid pectin
1–3 tsp rose water to taste

Prepare as for Apple and Ginger Jam (p. 139). Simmer the berries until tender, then crush with a spoon for a smoother set, if preferred.

ROCKIN' RASPBERRY JAM

This raspberry jam will rock your socks off in its pure and simple form, but for a spirited kick, add a shot or two of almond Amaretto or fruity kirsch liqueur. Then spoon into some home-baked jam tarts for tea with friends (see p. 117)

1.4 kg (3 lbs) raspberries
1.4 kg (3 lbs) sugar
2 tbsp liquid pectin
2–3 tbsp kirsch or amaretto (optional)

Prepare as for Apple and Ginger Jam (p. 139). Simmer the berries until tender, then crush with a spoon for a smoother set, if preferred.

ROLLICKIN' RHUBARB AND GINGER JAM

Rhubarb has a unique taste all on its own, but when paired with ginger and cinnamon, it acquires a sweet old-fashioned flavour and makes a delicate jam. Drizzle it on to piping hot porridge for a wicked weekend treat.

1.4 kg (3 lbs) rhubarb sticks,
cut into 5cm lengths
1.4 kg (3 lbs) sugar
2 tbsp liquid pectin
25 g (1 oz) fresh ginger,
grated or finely chopped
1 cinnamon stick (optional)

Prepare as for Apple and Ginger Jam (p. 139). Put the ginger in a muslin bag and put in the pan with the fruit and cinnamon stick, if using. Simmer until the fruit is soft but not entirely broken down.

MULLED PLUM JAM

This beautiful mulled jam is lovely at Christmas time and makes a perfect present. You can buy mulled wine tea bags from the supermarket for a spicy aromatic flavour.

1.4 kg (3 lbs) plums,
stoned and halved
½ tsp cloves
1 spiced mulled wine tea bag
1 cinnamon stick
Water to cover
1.4 kg (3 lbs) sugar
1 tbsp liquid pectin

Prepare as for Apple and Ginger Jam (p. 139). Put the stones, the cloves and the spiced mulled wine tea bag in a muslin bag and add to the pan with the fruit, cinnamon stick and water.

FLAVOUR OF THE MONTH

Experimenting with different taste combinations to create your own unique recipes is where you really get to go wild, so why not give your jam a little kick with a splash of kirsch or a punch of brandy for a drunken cherry or raspberry spin. Liqueurs make spirited accompaniments to fruit jams and can add an extra layer of complexity. Try amaretto, Kahlúa, Grand Marnier or Cointreau for a truly mean, mouth-watering marmalade. Any flavourings and liqueurs must be added at the end of the boiling process, after the jam has reached setting point, as it begins to cool down. If you add it earlier, the alcohol or essence will just burn off.

You could also use a combination of spices and other natural extracts such as vanilla pods, cinnamon sticks or even fresh ginger. Or why not add a tea bag or two to your pan to infuse calming chamomile or relaxing rosehip? Fresh herbs, like lavender, and flavoured waters, such as orange flower or rose water, make lightly perfumed potions to satisfy even the most epicurean of tastes. So stir up your imagination and invent your own fantasy flavours.

SEASONAL JAM CHART

	Apricots	Apples	Blackberries	Blackcurrants	Blood Oranges	Blueberries	Cherries	Clementines	Cranberries	Damsons	Figs	Gooseberries	Peaches	Pears	Plums	Raspberries	Redcurrants	Rhubarb	Satsumas	Seville Oranges	Strawberries
JAN					•	•														•	•
FEB					•																
MAR					•																
APR																					
MAY	•						•											•			
JUN	•					•	•									•					•
JUL	•		•	•								•				•	•				•
AUG	•	•	•	•						•			•		•						•
SEP		•	•	•						•	•		•	•	•	•					
OCT	•	•	•						•												
NOV	•							•	•										•		
DEC								•	•										•		

MARMALADE

Marmalade seems to have fallen out of favour with younger jam makers in recent years, perhaps because of a reputation for being old-fashioned and somewhat of an acquired taste. However, I've been enjoying it since I was a tiny tot – my grandmother used to (unbelievably) bottle-feed me Earl Grey tea, which I chased down with a round of marmalade on toast. She always used to say that getting the marmalade right would either make or break a breakfast. So forget everything you've heard: marmalade is delicious, a tangy alternative to the sugary sweetness of jam that will definitely help to wake you up in the morning. But there are many more uses for marmalade than just spreading on your breakfast toast (although that's the way I like it best): it can be used in your cakes, as a glaze for your roast dinner or to sharpen up a casserole. It's a preserve worth preserving and a welcome addition to any self-respecting jam maker's repertoire.

Marmalade in its simplest form is a jam made from citrus fruits like oranges, grapefruits, lemons and limes, either mixed together or singly. My grandmother, the marmalade connoisseur, used to liken choice of marmalade to that of jewellery – it ultimately comes down to personal taste. Delicate, chunky, clear set or cloudy, thick jewel-studded marmalade comes in a variety of shades and textures depending on the method of making.

Making marmalade only really differs from making jam in the addition of the rind and pith, which is included in long, slow simmering of the fruit. You'll also need to use larger quantities of water to cook the rinds until soft. All citrus fruits are naturally high in pectin, predominantly contained within the pith and the pips. These can be either tied up into a muslin bag and steeped in the pan or cooked directly into the jam after being ground up in a food processor with the fruit. The latter method results in a marmalade with a thicker cloudy texture, so if you're like me and prefer your marmalade crystal clear and finely cut, you will have to prepare yourself for a little more slicing and dicing.

FEED YOUR HEAD

I do like to think about what inspired the recipes that I dream up. For as long as I can remember, I have associated marmalade with *Alice in Wonderland*, probably because of the moment when Alice falls down the rabbit hole past the curious cupboards stocked with row upon row of various pots of preserves and jellies. My childhood memories of Alice, apart from the book, come from the 1988 cult classic stop-motion animation film *Alice*, by surrealist filmmaker Jan Svankmajer. If you haven't already seen it, rent the DVD now and explore Wonderland at its most crazy, cluttered and distorted. The caterpillar comes to life as an odd sock, the white rabbit stuffs his own stuffing and the mad March hare feverishly butters his pocket watch only to gobble it up afterwards. This is where my love affair with jam and marmalade began – I imagined myself as Alice, sampling curious cakes, potions and preserves – and today the story inspires me to conjure up my own recipes.

DOWN THE RABBIT HOLE MARMALADE

This marmalade recipe is as dark and heady as Grace Slick singing Jefferson Airplane's 'White Rabbit', given a treacly effect by the brown sugar. It is best served drizzled over a marmalade cake at high tea with friends.

1.4 kg (3 lbs) bitter oranges
(Seville or blood orange)
2 grapefruit
3.4 l (6 pints) water
2.7 kg (6 lbs) brown sugar
3 tbsp Grand Marnier

Wash and dry the fruit, cut in half and squeeze the juice into the pan. Remove the pith and pips and tie up in a muslin bag. Slice the remaining rind as thick or thin as you like and place in the pan with the muslin bag and the water. Simmer for about 1½ hours or until the rind has turned soft. Remove the muslin bag and squeeze any excess juice back into the pan. Add the sugar and stir until dissolved. Bring to a rapid rolling boil and cook until setting point is reached. Remove from the heat, skim off any scum and leave to cool for 10 minutes, to prevent the rind floating to the top of the jars. Add the Grand Marnier. Stir to distribute before funnelling into hot sterilized jars. Seal and cover.

OH MY DARLING CLEMENTINE MARMALADE

Clementines are much less bitter than the Seville oranges traditionally used for marmalade and make a lovely light alternative. Add a measure of Cointreau for an unconventional twist.

1.4 kg (3 lbs) clementines
2 lemons
3.4 l (6 pints) water
2.7 kg (6 lbs) sugar
3 tbsp Cointreau

Prepare as for Down the Rabbit Hole Marmalade above, adding the Cointreau before stirring and funnelling into jars.

TANGERINE DREAM MARMALADE

Buy tangerines when they are cheap and abundant at your local market and spread a little sunshine on to your toast with this truly dreamy marmalade.

1.4 kg (3 lbs) tangerines
2 lemons
2.8 l (5 pints) water
2 vanilla pods
2.3 kg (5 lbs) sugar

Prepare as for Down the Rabbit Hole Marmalade above. Slice the vanilla pods in half lengthwise, scrape the seeds into the pan and then add the pods to the rest of the ingredients.

STEAL THE LIMELIGHT LEMON AND LIME MARMALADE

Move over oranges, it's time for lemons and limes to sparkle, bringing a zingy freshness to the table. Lemons and limes are available all year round, so you can make this zesty marmalade whenever the urge strikes. Have it on toast or use it as a glaze for a dainty lemon cake.

450 g (1 lb) limes
900 g (2 lbs) lemons
3.4 l (6 pints) water
2.7 kg (6 lbs) sugar

Prepare as for Down the Rabbit Hole Marmalade above.

• CHUTNEY •

CHUTNEY is a CONDIMENT of FRUIT and VEGETABLES BOILED DOWN to a PULP WITH SUGAR, VINEGAR, SPICES and SALT.

Chutney is a condiment of fruit and vegetables boiled down to a pulp with sugar, vinegar, spices and salt. It is wonderfully aromatic, both sweet and sour, and if you haven't yet been captivated by chutney's charms, you quite simply don't know what you're missing. For years, I used to shrink away from the stuff – never having tasted it, I thought it seemed a fuddy-duddy sort of thing to eat. Then one day my taste buds woke up, when my sister threw a pot-luck cheese and wine party. I thought, well, if I can make jam, I can certainly have a go at chutney, and I set to work. I was an overnight convert and now I can't get enough of the stuff.

Making chutney is a seriously simple process, not that different from making jam but, like marmalade, requiring longer, slower cooking (anywhere from 2 to 4 hours) to blend the flavours and obtain a successful setting point. A food processor can be useful for cutting up large quantities of fruit and vegetables, especially if (like me) you prefer a smoother set. If, however, you prefer your chutney on the chunkier side, you'll have to use plenty of elbow grease to cut everything up into bite-sized pieces by hand. But trust me, it'll be well worth it in the end.

INGREDIENTS

SUGAR

You can use almost any type of sugar for making chutney, including white granulated or brown. I like to use a mixture (a great way to make use of leftover store-cupboard staples).

VINEGAR

Similarly, you can use almost any type of vinegar, including white vinegar, malt vinegar, cider vinegar and wine vinegar. Again, I often use a mixture. My favourite combination is half malt vinegar and half white vinegar, but feel free to use up whatever you have in the cupboard.

SPICES

All sorts of herbs and spices can be added to your chutney pot, and what you use will boil down to personal preference. The most popular include salt, peppercorns, paprika, allspice, cloves, cinnamon, cardamom, ginger, cayenne pepper and mustard seeds. Keep in mind that you can be much more heavy-handed with ingredients when making chutney than you can with jam or marmalade, so don't bother fussing with the muslin spice bags. Just throw everything directly into the pan and wait for your kitchen to become filled with the glorious scent of warm aromatic spices. Mmmmmm.

STORING

Chutney tastes better as it matures and can be kept for up to a year in a cool dry cupboard. Once opened, store in the fridge.

SWEET TOMATO CHUTNEY

GREEN TOMATO CHUTNEY

This is one of my favourite chutneys and can be used in place of ketchup as a delicious relish for sandwiches and burgers. Use tomatoes at the height of the season – when they are bright red, juicy and plump.

1.4 kg (3 lbs) ripe red tomatoes, diced
450 g (1 lb) cooking apples, peeled, cored and sliced
450 g (1 lb) onions or shallots, peeled and sliced
575 ml (1 pint) vinegar
450 g (1 lb) sugar
1 tbsp salt
2 tbsp mustard seeds
1 tbsp cayenne pepper

Put all the ingredients in the pan over a low heat, and stir until the sugar is completely dissolved. Bring to a furious boil, then turn the heat down and simmer for 1–2 hours or until the chutney has thickened to the desired consistency. Funnel into hot sterilized jars. Seal and cover.

———————

Green tomatoes are usually available at the end of the tomato season, and this recipe is great for using up unripe fruit that would otherwise be inedible.

1.4 kg (3 lbs) green tomatoes, diced
450 g (1 lb) cooking apples, peeled, cored and sliced
450 g (1 lb) onions or shallots, peeled and sliced
2 cloves garlic, crushed
575 ml (1 pint) vinegar
450 g (1 lb) sugar
1 tbsp salt
2 tbsp mustard seeds
25 g (1 oz) fresh ginger, peeled and finely chopped

Prepare as for Sweet Tomato Chutney (left).

———————

APPLE CHUTNEY

Sour cooking apples form the basis of this classic recipe, blending tangy British Bramleys with cinnamon, cloves and ginger: sweetness with a sprinkle of spice.

900 g (2 lbs) sour cooking apples, peeled, cored and sliced
450 g (1 lb) onions or shallots, peeled and sliced
450 g (1 lb) sultanas
25 g (1 oz) fresh ginger, peeled and finely chopped
450 g (1 lb) sugar
575 ml (1 pint) vinegar
1 tbsp salt
1 tsp allspice
1 tsp ground cloves
1 cinnamon stick

Prepare as for Sweet Tomato Chutney (opposite), removing the cinnamon stick before funnelling into jars.

PLUM CHUTNEY

This delicious autumn chutney can be made with any type of plum, including damsons.

1.4 kg (3 lbs) plums, stones removed
450 g (1 lb) onions or shallots, peeled and sliced
450 g (1 lb) cooking apples, peeled, cored and sliced
450 g (1 lb) sugar
575 ml (1 pint) vinegar
1 tbsp salt
25 g (1 oz) fresh ginger, peeled and finely chopped
1 tsp allspice
1 tsp ground cloves
1 cinnamon stick

Prepare as for Sweet Tomato Chutney (opposite), removing the cinnamon stick before funnelling into jars.

you've got it covered

Loves Me, Loves Me N...
ROSE PETAL JAM

MAKE JAM-JAR COVERS

Crafting your own jam-jar covers is an essential part of the jam-making fun, so raid your scrap bags and tie down your sealed pots of preserves with circles of festive fabric. Try colour coordinating to suit a theme or a holiday, or even the flavour of jam. And why not hand-embroider a ribbon with the recipient's name?

YOU WILL NEED:

Fabric scissors – preferably pinking shears
Scrap fabric
Double-sided Sellotape
Ribbons and ties – string, wire, raffia, bows, lace . . . anything goes
Embellishments – scraps of oilcloth, crochet or paper doilies, trinkets, little glass beads, ric rac

MAKING:

1. Cut out a circle of fabric at least 5 cm wider than your jar lid. Use pinking shears to trim a decorative edge that won't fray. Place the fabric circle on top of your lid, securing with a piece of double-sided tape.

2. Then secure again with a rubber band and your ribbon (or whatever you are using) wrapped around the neck of the jar, gathering the extra fabric.

3. Finally, tag your jams with some handmade labels (see right) and personalize with amusing inscriptions for friends and family.

★ ★

WORD UP!
MAKE YOUR OWN HOMEMADE LABELS

No pot of homemade jam, chutney or marmalade is complete without a handmade label to identify the deliciousness that waits inside, so jazz up your jars with unique and crafty tags. Personalize luggage labels with coloured pens, stencils, Letraset lettering or rubber stamps. Or cut out labels from some brightly coloured card or patterned paper, punch a hole, then tie round the neck of the jar with some string or pretty ribbon. If you're computer savvy, design some bold graphics to print on to sticky white labels bought from a stationery shop.

★ ★

• SPREAD THE LOVE •

Homemade jams, marmalades and chutneys make the most delicious gifts, and the giving and sharing of food is a time-honoured tradition as well as a thoughtful way of showing appreciation to friends and family. If you're planning on cooking up a big batch and are running low on recycled empties, as I often do, especially around the holidays (when demand outstrips supply), you can buy brand-new uniform jam jars from specialist shops or online (although this is more expensive and less green than reusing old jars). For cute polka-dot lidded jars, check **www.jamjarshop.com.**

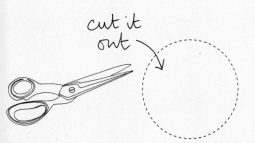

cut it out

Kitchen

ardening

Kitchen Gardening

It's impossible for you not to have noticed that there's a back-to-basics food revival going on, and a resurgence of interest in gardening has taken root too, as more and more people want to eat fresh, locally grown and seasonal foods. But for those of us who are urbanites and apartment-dwellers, outside space is a luxury and allotment waiting lists now span decades. The good news, though, is that you really don't need outside space to get crafty with your gardening gloves. For years, I lived just off a busy main road that connected the City to the mean streets of East London. Traffic thundered past my window day and night. My gardening fantasies seemed exactly that until I thought of new ways to get my green-fingered kicks.

Digging Up History

Throughout the ages, women have known how to grow domestic plants and herbs – keeping both the kitchen store cupboard and the medicine cabinet stocked. Luckily for us, these gardening goddesses were careful to hand down their folk wisdom (today, plant extracts are still used in many beauty products; see pp. 183–93 for some natural beauty recipes to keep you feeling fresh as a daisy). Women have also known that a little dirt never hurt – the gutsy girls of the Women's Land Army rolled up their sleeves and kept food on British tables during wartime. This down-to-earth attitude helped women break new ground, much like the guerrilla gardeners of today who cultivate plants to transform public spaces and pimp up pavements. Way to grow, guys!

Born to Be Wild

Using minimal space means seizing even unconventional or unexpected opportunities to cultivate your urban oasis. Creativity and imagination will become part of your everyday gardening armoury. So if your home is lacking in greenery, why not take a walk on the wild side and discover how much fun it is to get growing? Try colouring carnations in a rainbow hue (p. 171) or plant a victory herb garden (p. 158). You'll soon see that not having a garden to call your own doesn't have to leave you green with envy of those who can more easily indulge their horticultural urges. Find out what a thrill it is to watch something grow, knowing that you've been involved in the process from seed to sprout – and you'll also feel reconnected to the food you eat.

WAY TO GROW, GUYS!

Sprouting the Seeds of a Revolution

The easiest way to grow greens at home is to germinate raw seeds by soaking, draining and rinsing them until they sprout roots or leaves that are good to eat. My granny taught me this oh-so-simple skill. When times were tough, she would sprout seeds and sell them to the hippies at the famous flea markets in Ibiza. This money-making scheme fitted in perfectly with her party-girl lifestyle – even if she had been out dancing on tables all night, she could still race home at dawn to water her baby plants. And this is one reason why I love sprouting seedlings so much – for minimum effort you get maximum reward.

Sprouted seeds are absolutely loaded with energy, not to mention power-packed with essential nutrients, vitamins and minerals. The packets you've probably seen in the supermarket or in health food stores are expensive and once opened, the seedlings don't stay fresh for very long. So it's great to know that you can grow them yourself at home for next to nothing. Raw seeds and beans are extremely cheap and will last you at least a year, if not two, as long as you store them in airtight containers.

You can sprout almost any type of seed or bean and even some nuts, but some are not that nice to eat and one or two have potentially harmful side effects, like kidney beans and tomato seeds. So please always read up on anything new before you try sprouting it. Here's a list of safe seeds and beans to grow, which are popular for both their flavour and their sproutability:

- aduki beans • mung beans • chick peas
- brown lentils • alfalfa seeds
- radish seeds

Well, actually, you don't have to! Yep, you heard me. You don't need a garden, a patio or a roof terrace to get gardening. Hell, you don't even need a window box. Okay, a sunny window ledge might help things along but if I was able to cultivate plants in my small sunless London flat, you can too, no matter where you live. I will show you how to become an indoor gardening guru in the comfort of your own kitchen. Join the home-grown food revolution, and save a bit of money too!

Learning a few basic techniques to grow your own sustainable salad box at home will mean you'll always have fresh nutritious ingredients to hand. And nothing is as satisfying as watching something you planted with your own hands grow and getting to eat it afterwards.

YOU WILL NEED:

1. Sprouting seeds – you need just 1 tablespoon of seed to make a jar of sprouts. Buy organic where possible, as they contain fewer pesticides and chemicals. Packets of raw seeds and beans can be bought in special sprouting packs from good supermarkets and health food stores.

2. Sprouting container – you can buy nifty sprouting trays fairly cheaply from garden centres and health food stores. However, a Kilner jar (large rubber-sealed, screw-topped glass jar used for preserves) will do just as well and is the ideal size and shape. Failing that, any large, wide-mouthed glass jar will do the job. You'll need to use a different jar or tray for each seed or bean you are going to sprout – clean it thoroughly before use to prevent mould or bacteria contaminating the seedlings.

3. Muslin and rubber bands – to cover the jars. The muslin allows air in, which the seedlings need to germinate. Never put a lid on to your sprout jar or you'll suffocate your seedlings!

4. Fresh water – use filtered or purified water if possible, but tap water is fine. If you are happy to drink the water, your seedlings will be too.

HOW TO SPROUT:

From small beginnings come great things. Follow these step-by-step instructions and watch as a whole garden magically grows from a humble tablespoon of seed. Sprouted seedlings will be ready to eat within 3–5 days.

READY, SET, GROW!

1. Give your chosen seeds or beans a good rinse in a sieve to get rid of any dirt, dust or pesticides. Then soak in a large bowl of water overnight or for at least 8 hours.

2. After draining, put the soaked seeds or beans in your jar and fill to just a little over halfway up with fresh water. The general rule is one part seed to three parts water. (A tablespoon may seem a very small amount, but trust me, the seeds will double in size as they sprout so they need a lot of room to expand.) Cut a square of muslin large enough to cover the mouth of the jar with an overhang and secure with a rubber band.

3. Put the jar somewhere out of direct sunlight (which will encourage the growth of mould). I leave mine in the kitchen on a shelf by the sink. If you can't find a dark enough spot, place a tea towel over the jar. Leave overnight.

4. The next day, while you're having your morning tea or coffee, drain off the water in the jar, refill with fresh water and rinse the sprouts by gently swilling and swishing them around in the jar. Keep the muslin on at all times – the water can flow in and out but the seeds can't fall out. Drain the water again, then place the jar tilted at a 45° angle, mouth down, either on a drying rack by the sink or propped up in a bowl.

5. Repeat step 4 twice daily, morning and evening, for the next three days. On day 4, after you have given the sprouts their morning rinse, place the jar where it will get some indirect sunlight – this will cause the sprouts to make some chlorophyll, which will green them up a little.

6. Continue rinsing twice daily until the sprouts are ready to eat (see p. 156). It's as simple as that!

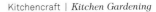

HOW TO TELL WHEN THE SEEDLINGS ARE READY TO EAT

As the seedlings germinate, they start to grow little tail-like roots (some seeds even grow small green leaves). The sprouted seedlings are ready to eat when the tails are at least 1 cm long. Give them a final rinse, drain off the water and transfer the jar to the fridge, where they can be kept for up to a week. When the sprouted seedlings begin to smell bad or turn brown, toss them in the bin, or better yet the compost, and start the process all over again for more sprouted goodness.

SAVE YOUR RINSE WATER!

Use your sprouted seedlings' energy-infused rinse water as homemade fertilizer to feed your houseplants.

CRESS AND MUSTARD POTS

Other microgreens, like mustard and cress, can be just as fun and satisfying to grow – and as tasty. You'll probably remember doing this at school during your own salad days. The best thing about growing cress and mustard heads is that you get to make your own kitsch containers from recycled plastic pots. Mustard seedlings have a peppery bite so are great for using as a garnish, whereas cress seedlings taste milder and work brilliantly in salads. If you like to mix things up a bit, you can grow them together in the same pot, but sow the mustard seeds first (they take longer to germinate) and add in the cress about 3 days later. You can buy the seeds from a good supermarket or garden centre.

YOU WILL NEED:

- EMPTY YOGURT POTS OR ANY OTHER SMALL PLASTIC CONTAINER
- MUSTARD OR CRESS SEEDS
- COTTON WOOL BALLS
- ACRYLIC PAINT AND PAINTBRUSH
- NEWSPAPER
- SPRAY BOTTLE FILLED WITH PURIFIED WATER
- SUNNY WINDOW LEDGE

HOW TO SPROUT:

First the fun part – decorating your pots. Peel the labels off your empty pots, and clean and dry them thoroughly. Spread out your newspaper. Paint the pots however you like, perhaps coordinating with the colours of your kitchen. When the paint has dried, decorate with whatever you fancy – stick on some eye-lashed goggle eyes, draw funny faces or bedazzle with some plastic gems. The more outrageous the better!

Now you are ready to sow your seeds. Make sure your hands are thoroughly clean before you begin, as you don't want any bacteria spoiling the seeds' growth. Then ...

cress pots

1 Lightly dampen the cotton wool with your spray bottle and place enough into the bottom of the pot to reach about 2 cm below the top. Evenly sprinkle a generous handful of seeds on to the damp cotton wool – try not to let them clump together too much. Press them down lightly into the cotton wool.

2 Leave on a warm window ledge and watch the magic happen. Spritz the seeds with water whenever the cotton wool feels dry to the touch (I check mine once a day). You want to keep them moist but not too wet.

3 When the shoots are at least 5 cm tall (this will take 7–15 days), they are ready to harvest. Snip them with a pair of kitchen scissors just above the root, rinse in a sieve and enjoy!

Grow Your Own Victory Herb Garden

Back in the 40s, as war-torn Britain reached a food shortage crisis, rationing was introduced and the 'Dig for Victory' campaign encouraged the nation to grow their own, supplementing food rations with fresh home-grown produce. Posters, booklets and leaflets provided all the know-how to empower the people with morale-boosting gardening skills.

Retrospectively, it has been said that the British public never ate so well, as all over the country, mini allotments sprang up on lawns and flowerbeds, wasteland and rooftops. Even public land was transformed, including Hyde Park, famously home to one of London's largest victory gardens.

No need to contemplate lengthy waiting lists for an allotment, or risk a criminal record for digging up next door's flowerbeds; instead, cultivate your own victory herb garden in your kitchen. Strong and hardy herb plants can easily be grown indoors as they need little pandering to. If you're a beginner, it's easier to plant a container with pre-grown potted plants (growing herbs from scratch is not always possible; sowing at the wrong time could mean your best-laid plans go to pot).

Plus you don't need so much light and space – this is how I grew plants in my dark little flat. I bought small baby herbs from the market, potted them in customized containers and watched them grow into happy healthy plants. Perfect – fresh edible produce year-round. Now let's get growing!

Container – half the fun of planting a herb garden is choosing containers to pot your plants in. Old-fashioned fruit crates, wine boxes, gardening trugs, buckets, cans, biscuit tins and teapots are all great for containing and displaying your home-grown herbs. If you want to splash out on something a little special, check out the personalized crates you can buy from www.notonthehighstreet.com. There are two factors you should keep in mind when choosing a container:

DRAINAGE – all living plants need to be watered, but the water must be able to drain away or you may have problems with pests or, worse, root rot. The simple solution is to make a few holes in the base of your container and stand it in a dish or a tray. Alternatively, pot your plants in standard plastic plant pots, then arrange them inside fancy crates. The ultimate no-fuss solution is to buy a brand-new plastic container from your local garden centre, which may not be as pretty but will have built-in drainage.

SIZE – the container must be deep enough to comfortably hold your chosen plants and allow them room to grow. Anywhere from about 15 to 30 cm deep should be adequate.

Herbs – buy your herb plants from a market, garden centre or nursery. What you choose to grow entirely depends on what you like to eat. But start small. If you begin with just 3 or 4 different herbs you love, you will be less likely to neglect your garden. As you get more experienced, you can experiment with new and unfamiliar herbs. Always look for strong healthy-looking plants and avoid any limp- or sickly-looking stragglers with pale or discoloured leaves. They should have a good general overall shape, not too small (which might indicate stunted growth) and not too large (which may mean the plant is overgrown and won't adapt well to repotting). See box, below, for plants that I grow and know thrive indoors.

Potting Soil – buy regular potting compost from your local garden centre.

Gravel – or small stones or pebbles, to line the base of your container.

Decorative paraphernalia – this is where you get to use your imagination. Dress up your box with plant markers and labels or add some mini paper bunting for a vintage touch (see p. 161).

WHICH HERB?

BASIL A robust Mediterranean herb that prefers a sunny windowsill.

CHIVES Can be tricky to get going but will grow well on a shaded windowsill with plenty of watering.

CORIANDER A versatile herb that does well indoors. It has large roots, so will need a deep container with good drainage.

MINT A feisty grower that will try to bully other plants by taking over the entire container. Trim it regularly.

OREGANO A low-maintenance plant that does well indoors in a sunny, dry location.

ROSEMARY A strong hardy decorative plant that grows well under almost any conditions. It has large roots, so plant in a deep container.

PARSLEY A good low-maintenance plant that will grow well in a sunny spot.

SAGE A hardy and tolerant plant that does like some light, so position on a sunny windowsill.

THYME A hardy easy-to-care-for plant that can withstand the cold. Do not overwater.

HOW TO PLANT:

Okay, here comes the messy part. If you don't want to wreck your house, it's best to do this outside. Indoors, make sure you use loads of newspaper to cover your workspace before you begin. As soon as you get your hand-picked herb plants home, water them and get them potted – if you leave them in their temporary plastic pots for too long, their roots will become stunted. Then . . .

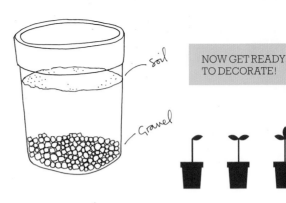

soil

Gravel

NOW GET READY
TO DECORATE!

1. Line your clean container with a handful of gravel, stones or pebbles, which will allow the plants to drain when watered. Fill to 2–3 cm from the top with potting soil – don't pack it too tightly, or the roots won't have room to grow.

2. Figure out where you want to place each plant within the container (you don't want to squash them too close together, so leave about 10 cm between them) and make small wells with your hands where you want them to go.

3. Remove your herb plants from their temporary pots by holding the plant by the base and tilting it down at a 45° angle while slowly teasing off the pot. Place the plants roots down into the small wells and press down on the soil around the plant, adding a bit more if needed until they sit snugly in the earth.

The **position** of your plant pot or container will be key to the success of your herb garden. If you're making one for culinary purposes, you will probably want it close to your cooking area. A sunny kitchen windowsill is ideal but if you don't have one, don't worry. A well-positioned table or a ledge with indirect sunlight will do just as well.

Water your plants immediately and continue to do so on a regular basis. Don't just water your plants as and when you feel like it. Overwatering is the kiss of death, as the water will stagnate and a nasty bout of root rot or an infestation of pests may set in. Conversely, if your plants are too dry, they will begin to wilt and die. Watering once a week is usually enough, but **use your initiative:** test the soil with your hands, and if it still feels moist, wait until it begins to dry out before you water again. And remember: in the hotter months, the soil will dry out quicker and you will probably have to water your plants more often.

DISH THE DIRT – *Seed Markers*

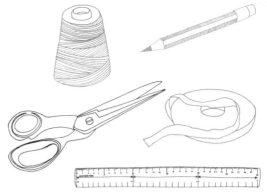

Markers to identify the herbs in your mini garden are not only useful but fun to make too. Use wooden lollipop sticks – if you can get your hands on the jumbo variety, so much the better, as you will have more room to tag your home-grown herbs. Failing that, wooden forks from the chip shop would do. You can even make your own from recycled plastics: wash and dry thoroughly before cutting out into your preferred shape and size – say 15 cm, to allow a good 5 cm to sit in the earth.

PAPER BUNTING

Spruce up your victory garden with this patriotic paper bunting. Customize to fit your chosen container. I like to string mine as a backdrop for my victory garden crate.

YOU WILL NEED:

DECORATIVE PAPER
RULER AND PENCIL
SCISSORS
STRING
DOUBLE-SIDED SELLOTAPE
WOODEN SKEWERS
OR STICKS

1. Use your ruler to mark out diamonds with 6cm sides on your paper and cut out enough to fit the length of your victory garden (you can draw and cut out one, then use that as a template). Fold your diamonds in half so the top and bottom tips meet for the triangular flags.

2. Cut a length of string long enough to accommodate all the flags, with 5–8 cm extra at either end for tying.

3. To attach the flags to the string, place each flag so that the string is contained within the flap, then stick down with a small piece of double-sided tape. Leave some room at the fold (about 0.5 cm) so they can easily be repositioned along the string garland.

4. Make a loop at each end of your string, then tie on to the wooden sticks. Plant firmly into the soil of your victory garden.

TIMING IS EVERYTHING! GROW PLANTS FROM SEED

You generally have only one window of opportunity to grow most seedlings from scratch, and that's during the spring, when the weather is mild enough but not too hot for the seeds to germinate successfully. Invest in a plastic seed tray and line it with some special seed-sowing compost (you can buy both from your local garden centre). Sprinkle your chosen seeds evenly and sparsely over the surface, cover with another layer of compost and water sparingly. Cover the tray with a glass top (which you can purchase from a glass shop) until the seedlings begin to show. Germination can take weeks or even months, so with seed planting, patience is most definitely a virtue!

HAVE FUN IN THE MUD – VOLUNTEER

If you fancy doing some real get-your-hands-dirty gardening but lack the ground space, why not volunteer at an urban farm or community garden? If you are able to lend a helping hand a few hours a week, you could offer your time in exchange for learning some new skills.

one Lump

OR

Sugar Cube.

Plant a Tea Garden

Who doesn't like a refreshing cup of mint tea? Use your new planting skills to grow a tea garden, and before long you'll be making your own unique home-brewed herbal teas, tisanes and infusions. Host a tea party and serve your home-grown herbal teas with some delicious homemade cakes and biscuits (see 'Baking', p. 28). To make your teas, you can either use the herbs fresh, straight out of the ground, or allow the leaves to dry out for a few days before crushing and then infusing (see p. 166). You could even try your hand at making your own tea bags. Have fun experimenting to create unique blends, then fill muslin spice bags with your chosen combinations and store in airtight containers.

Always do your research and read up on any new herbs you want to try out before using. Here's a list of herbs that I like to grow and use at home:

LEMON BALM
The leaves of this plant make a tea that helps to promote sleep and relieve stress, and is also good for warding off seasonal coughs and colds.

LEMON VERBENA
Makes a soothing lemon tea, which can aid digestion. Add a cinnamon stick to the pot for warmth and to restore low energy.

CHAMOMILE
The small white flowers of this popular herb make the most gloriously calming tea that can help soothe and settle the nerves. It doesn't grow very well indoors, so should be planted in a sunny window box outside.

GARDEN MINT
One of the most popular herbs to grow, it makes a wonderfully soothing tea that can aid digestion.

PEPPERMINT
Also a good digestive, peppermint is both warming and cooling – great for when you're feeling under the weather.

How to Make a Tea Infusion

Create your own delicious and therapeutic tea blends from your home-grown herbs by simply steeping them in hot water. Just as if you were making a regular loose-leaf cup of tea, put your herbs in a strainer in either a mug or a teapot and top with hot water before leaving for about 5–10 minutes. If you've opted for dried herbs, use 1 tsp per cup of water. For fresh herbs, use at least 2 tsp per cup of water.

To make iced tea, prepare as above before pouring into glasses one-third full of crushed ice. Add sugar to taste, a slice of lemon and a leaf of mint. For an extra sweet touch, make some lemon sugar by rubbing sugar cubes against the rind of a zested lemon, then store in an airtight jar for a few hours before serving with your herbal infusions.

How to Dry Herbs

Cut herbs at the base of the stem with a pair of scissors. Once you've gathered enough, either put them in a paper bag or wrap them up in some kitchen towel, then leave to dry in a warm, dark, well-ventilated room for at least 2 days (an airing cupboard would be ideal). The herbs are ready when they feel dry and crumbly to touch. Once dried, crumble them into an airtight container to store. Then use in your cooking, infusions or for herb sachets and bags (see opposite).

To dry lavender, pick off about 10–15 cm of stalk, including the purple flower heads (the lovely scented bit), tie them together with some string and hang upside down in a warm, dark, dry place (again, an airing cupboard would be perfect). Leave for at least a week before using. Use to make some lovely lavender-infused sugar (see p. 124).

HERBS MAKE GOOD SCENTS –
MAKE YOUR OWN SCENTED BAGS

Use your home-dried herbs to make sweet-smelling fragrance bags to ward off moths and keep your clothes and linens smelling garden-fresh. If you're like me and love vintage garb, you'll know that sourcing pre-loved retro threads in second-hand shops, flea markets and car boot sales means risking moths. In the past, these flighty fellows have not only made lunch out of my winter woollies and chomped their way through countless cashmere treasures but also followed me around as I moved from house to house. Never one to opt for the chemical solution (especially as the safety of traditional mothballs has been questioned in recent years), I prefer the botanical route of moth-ridding by sewing my own sweetly scented herb bags. The great thing is that although they smell repellent to the moths, they smell deliciously fragrant to us. And guess what – they really do work! Keep them in your drawers and cupboards or hang up in the wardrobe to keep your clothes smelling fresh and moth-free. Make your bags as plain or as decorative as you like, with beads, ribbon or a touch of lace.

YOU WILL NEED:

DRIED HERBS – just a handful for each sachet. Use a selection of dried herbs, spices and essential oils, such as lavender, rosemary, thyme, mint, cloves, cinnamon sticks (cut into small pieces), dried citrus fruit peel, cedarwood oil or lavender oil (which moths find particularly repellent), or keep it simple and stick to just lavender. Lavender bags double up as dreamy sleepy pillows, inducing calm at bedtime.

BOWL

2 X FABRIC SQUARES, 10 X 10 CM – a loose-weave breathable porous fabric like linen, hessian, calico or light cotton would be ideal.

SCISSORS OR PINKING SHEARS

SEWING MACHINE OR NEEDLE AND THREAD

MAKING:

1. Crumble your dried herbs and strip any flowers from the stems by pulling your fingers down along the buds until they fall off. Put them in a bowl with any spices and essential oils you are using (a good dash of oil will do). You could add some dried flowers to bulk it up or some dried beans to add some weight.

2. Decorate one of the squares – sew on some pretty ribbon, lace or even an appliqué heart. You could even use fabric paint and stamps to create stencilled designs.

3. Line up the two squares with right sides (the front of the fabric) facing together and sew around three of the four edges either by hand using a backstitch (see p. 61) or on the machine using a straight stitch and a 1cm seam allowance (see p. 76). Leave the fourth seam open for filling. Turn the pocket right side out and use a long blunt object like a pencil or knitting needle to work the corners into sharp points.

4. Fill the bag with your dried herb mixture, making sure you don't overstuff (or you'll find it difficult to sew the final seam shut). Tuck in the final seam and sew the opening closed by hand with a slipstitch (see p. 62) or gather together and tie shut with a length of ribbon, trimming the edges with pinking shears for a cute no-fray finish.

5. Your sweet-smelling sachets will last for about a year, but are only as effective as the potency of their scent, which will fade over time. To top up the aroma, sprinkle a few drops of some lavender or cedarwood essential oil on to the fabric bag.

Fragrance in a bag

GET POTTY –
CREATIVE PLANT POTTING

Shop-bought garden containers are costly and, more often than not, downright boring, which is why I like to customize mine by decorating old tin cans, paint pots and any other useful container that might usually be discarded. Let your imagination run wild when choosing your decorative coverings – try sticky-backed vinyl (a favourite of mine, as it's an absolute dream to use). Chamomile plants, with their big cheerful daisy heads, always look darling when matched with leopard-print vinyl – sure to add some kitsch to your kitchen. Or give a gift to the dandelion dude in your life – plant some wild weeds in an old tin can covered in some manly faux bois (fake wood).

MAKING:

1. Clean your tin can or paint pot (or whatever container you have chosen) thoroughly and remove any traces of the lid or labels. If the label is still intact, put aside to use later as a template for your decorative cover.

2. Bang a few drainage holes in the bottom of your container with the hammer and nail. Just be careful of your fingers!

3. Measure the height and circumference of your container so you know how big to make your covering. (If you removed the label intact, use that as a template.) Mark the rectangle in the required dimensions on to the wrong side of your chosen covering and cut out.

4. If you're using sticky-backed vinyl, all you have to do is stick it directly on to the can. If you're using fabric, oilcloth or paper, use a strong craft glue to stick it on to the container, smoothing it down as you go, and then set aside to dry.

5. Line the bottom of your container with a small handful of pebbles or gravel and fill it up with potting soil to about 1 cm from the top. Make a small well in the soil in the middle of the pot. Carefully remove your plant from its temporary plastic pot by holding it close to the roots and tilting it at a 45° angle. Place your plant in the well and firm the soil around it, adding a little more if needed. Water immediately and place to be admired on a sunny window ledge.

drainage holes
in the bottom
of tins

hammer
time

MAKE A MINI GARDEN TABLE DECORATION

Believe it or not, I was a champion miniature-garden landscaper at school. Something about gardening in miniature appealed to my sense of fantasy and I won just about every competition running. So it's safe to say I am more than delighted to see it come back in vogue in recent years. Fancy florists are now asking budget-busting prices for darling table decorations and charming centrepieces. But really, why pay money for something you can easily create yourself at home for next to nothing? Gardening in miniature is buckets of fun and the best thing about it is that you need zero gardening skills or know-how to pull it off. All you really need is an empty afternoon, a couple of plants, some potting soil, a handful of decorations and, most importantly, your imagination – your garden can be as fantastical as you like. Pick a theme – holiday seasons are always a fun excuse to make a poinsettia paradise or an Easter Arcadia complete with mini chocolate eggs and fluffy chicks. Why not create a fairy grotto, an octopus's garden or a Shangri-La of wonder, magic and whimsy? The more bonkers the better, I say! Miniature gardens make the most amazing table decorations – a sure-fire conversation starter for dinner parties.

YOU WILL NEED:

A CONTAINER – nothing too big or unwieldy; a ceramic bowl or something that will look nice on the centre of the table works best. I often use a spare mixing bowl, but really anything goes, so scour your cupboards or local charity shops.

SMALL PLANTS AND FLOWERS – any kind of miniature blooms, dwarf plants or even cacti will work well. Moss is perfect for masquerading as grass. Use anything that stays small, fits in with your theme and appeals to your sense of style. You can probably pick up most of the greenery you need on a country walk, a visit to the park or, if you live by the seaside, try combing the beach for some natural nautical treasures.

DECORATIONS AND OBJECTS – let your imagination fly: rocks, twigs, figurines, cake decorations, cocktail umbrellas, doll's house furniture; again, anything goes as long as it's small. No need to go out and buy anything new either; take a look around the house for inspiration, or better yet, go for a walk and collect some natural materials for your garden – it's free!

TOOLS – scissors, spoons and forks all make perfect mini gardening tools.
POTTING SOIL
SPRAY WATER BOTTLE
NEWSPAPER

MAKING:

Before you begin, decide what kind of scene or theme you want to create and select your container to suit. Remember, if you're planning on including living plants in your design, you will need drainage holes and a dish or a saucer for the container to sit in. Cover your workspace with newspaper and we can get gardening.

1. Fill your container with potting soil to 2–3 cm from the top. Decide where you want to place your plants within your design and make little wells in the soil. Now pot the taller plants first, then the smaller, shorter ones. Give them a little water at this stage.

2. Then let your imagination run wild! Make a moss lawn, build mini hills to give a sense of scale and height, lay gravel paths or plant trees made from twigs. Continue to make adjustments as you go along until you're happy with the finished design. This is the fun part, so take your time.

3. Now add your extra ornaments for attention-grabbing embellishment. Go as gaudy as you like for a truly fantastical feel.

4. When your garden is finished, place it in prime position on a table or tie a ribbon round it and give it to a friend. To keep your garden fresh, spritz it daily with a water bottle.

Petal Power – Flower Arranging for the Wild Child

Now this is throw-the-rulebook-out flower arranging. Forget everything you ever thought you knew about it. Arranging flowers is not an art that has to be taught – literally anyone can do it. One of the best things about flowers is their forgiving nature, so go wild and experiment. Use blossoms from the garden, or collect them for free. Pick weeds and wildflowers or make like my grandmother, who isn't above snipping off bits and pieces at the roadside. She often walks about with a pair of scissors in hand, hunting for illicit treasures – her rule is anything that's spilling or hanging on to the street is fair game.

If you don't fancy getting caught red-handed, visit a local market, the next best place to get hold of cheap and cheerful blooms. My favourite place to go is Columbia Road flower market, where you can snap up blooming bargains late on Sunday afternoon. Check out your local florist too – they often get rid of stuff long before it really needs to be binned. Odd bits of greenery, leaves, woody stems and branches can have their own messy charm when mixed in with more traditional floral designs.

The secret to long-lasting flower arrangements is to pick your flowers before they hit their prime. And always cut their stems at an angle, then immediately stand in a vase of cold water to give them a long drink and get them looking their best. Remove any straggly leaves or damaged petals before putting into your arrangement, and change the water every few days. Leaving your flowers submerged in cloudy water will only encourage bacteria, which will kill off your beautiful blossoms. A teaspoon of sugar in the water helps the flowers bloom for longer too.

When arranging your flowers, think about balance, scale, colour and contrast, but don't be afraid to mix it up and make bold statements with clashing colours. You could even try tie-dyeing white flowers for some real vibrancy (see right). And don't forget that fake is fun too – plastic flower garlands from the pound shop woven with fairy lights will brighten up a gloomy corner. Or try making a bunch of paper flowers (like the tissue paper roses on p. 231) to beautify your space.

Get inventive with your containers and vases – for table decorations, try arranging flowers in cast-off crockery, milk jugs or old teapots. My favourite vase is a gorgeous chintzy old coffee pot that I started using for flowers because I broke its lid and hadn't the heart to throw it out. Luckily, it looks divine crammed full of daffodils or sprouting a bunch of spring tulips. Small and simple decorations can often make just as big an impact – a stub of roses in a jam jar or a handful of flowers in a supermarket berry punnet or miniature trug. Or spray-paint an old plastic container, or even recycle wine bottles, which look lovely matched with a single flower. Not forgetting floating flowers: pick out a pretty bowl, line with marbles or glass pebbles (pick them up in the florist), then fill with water and strew with carefully cut flower heads and a couple of floating tea lights.

SEIZE THE DAISIES – TIE-DYE FLOWERS

White flowers like daises, carnations and roses can easily be tinted with food colouring. Just cut the stems at an angle and submerge the ends in a glass of water tinted with a pot of food dye (generally red or blue works best). Leave for 24 hours – the dye is magically drawn up and absorbed into the petals. Remove the flowers from the water and run the stems under the tap before placing in a vase of clean water.

For multi-coloured tie-dyeing, split the end of the flower stem into several sections, then place each section into a separate glass of differently coloured water (you may need to prop the flower up while it is absorbing the colours). Leave for 24 hours, then remove the flower and rinse the stem under the tap before trimming down and placing in a vase for a blooming marvellous effect.

PART 3

HOME

DIY BEAUTY • MA
&

CRAFT

GATHERINGS

CANDY PINK

PEPPERMINT FOOT SCRUB

Get Spangled GLITTER GEL

POWDER PINK

DIYBEAUTY

DIY
beauty

Homemade bath, beauty and cosmetic products are not only fun to make but are great for your skin too. Your skin is your largest organ, and what you put on it is vital for keeping it both looking and feeling great. Commercial products may appear to offer great benefits, but don't be fooled by glossy packaging and seductive marketing ploys with provocative promises that sound too good to be true – more often than not they are. Many of these so called miracle creams contain only very small amounts of their active ingredients (the stuff that actually makes a difference) – the rest can be made up of all sorts of synthetic nasties, including mountains of preservatives and even some potentially damaging chemicals, all of which can disrupt the natural balance of our bodies.

Which is bad news if you're anything like my sister, who has such highly sensitive skin she can use hardly any shop-bought products without disastrous side effects. So if you suffer from allergies or sensitive skin, when it comes to your beauty routine, homemade is better than ready-made. Just think about it this way: we wouldn't dare eat or drink half of the chemicals listed in most beauty products, yet we don't think twice about smothering them all over our skin to be absorbed into our bodies through our pores.

BE YOUR OWN BEAUTY EXPERT

BECAUSE WE'RE WORTH IT

Growing up, I was practically forbidden from using commercially produced products – my mother, a committed naturopath and die-hard boho to the bone, banned my sister and me from using anything that wasn't 100% natural and chemical free.

Natural ingredients have been used on the skin for centuries, long before beauty became big business. The ancient Egyptians are credited with concocting the very first cosmetics, experimenting with minerals and charcoal to make eye-shadows and eyeliners. Yet throughout history, women have risked their health in the name of beauty: the fashion for very pale skin during the reign of Elizabeth I had women covering their faces with toxic lead-based powders and paints, while legendary Hollywood 'blonde bombshell' Jean Harlow was rumoured to have been fatally poisoned by her platinum hair dye.

Now, I know we've come a long way since then and beauty products are unlikely to kill you, but you should still be wary of chemically overloaded products. Get into the habit of reading labels, and make sure you read between the lines. The 'natural' beauty industry is surprisingly unregulated, and some of these products are actually not chemical free. Of course, there are some great products available but they often carry budget-busting price tags. Now here comes the good news! You needn't be priced out of the beauty game – luckily it's super easy to create your own beauty supplies at home. And for a fraction of the price too, since you often need look no further than your kitchen cupboard or bathroom cabinet. So why not break the mould, grab an apron and get ready to have some fun creating your own customized skincare products?

She would whip round our bedrooms when we were asleep and bin anything she deemed chemically dubious. So, while all my girlfriends were experimenting with the latest Impulse du jour, I was at home dabbling in the fine art of rose-petal stewing, trying to alchemize my way to smelling a million dollars, or at least as good as a bottle of Charlie Red. Needless to say, I rarely succeeded and was usually left with countless bottles of decaying flowers smelling about as rosy as a compost heap. Yet all was not lost, as it did spark a lifelong interest in DIY beauty. I still love crafting my own luscious lotions and personalized potions, preferring to steer clear of shop-bought products tested on animals or anything else harmful to the environment and the body as well. And why pay big bucks when you can so easily create homemade treatments and tonics? You owe it to yourself to become your own beauty expert, and you'll always be able to sort out unsightly blemishes or cheer up winter-worn chapped lips. But the best thing about brewing your own lotions and potions is that you get to stamp your identity on to your products, using the scents that you love and which suit you best.

You can buy many of the ingredients you will need from most good health stores, chemists and even supermarkets. However, if you prefer to source all your natural home-beauty goodies from a one-stop shop, there are also a number of great online retailers that sell all the specialist ingredients and equipment you will need (see 'Address Book', p. 235).

STORE-CUPBOARD INGREDIENTS

These are things you probably have already, in your fridge, store cupboard or bathroom cabinet. Sea salt and granulated sugar form the base for gorgeous exfoliating body scrubs that can rival even the most expensive brands. And bathroom cabinet regulars like Epsom and Dead Sea salts work beautifully combined with cooking oils to create intensely moisturizing scrubs. Plain old oats and ground almonds are yummy in baking but can also be a scrumptious addition to face masks and facial scrubs. You can even use some fruits and vegetables in your natural skincare preparations; lemons, bananas and avocados all have therapeutic properties and help soothe and heal tired or damaged skin and hair. Cider vinegar is renowned for its natural toning properties, and a squirt in a homemade toner will help get your skin soft and smooth.

Good old-fashioned cooking oils are also useful – both olive and avocado oil are gloriously moisturizing for the body as well as the face. My grandmother swears by this and has been oiling up her face like a Sunday roast for years (she looks pretty good for her age too). And Sophia Loren herself famously stated that this was her beauty secret. But my favourite kitchen ingredient of all time has got to be clear honey, long reputed to have healing powers. Manuka honey is especially luxurious, although it can be pricey (but a pot will last you some time, so in the long run it may be worth the splurge). It is legendary that Cleopatra would bathe in milk and honey to keep her skin looking young and beautiful – if it was good enough for the queen of Egypt, it's good enough for me and you!

NATURAL BEESWAX

As a thickening agent, beeswax is an integral component in most cosmetics, branded and homemade. You can buy either cakes or granules. Granules are easier to weigh out, but if you can only get hold of a cake, don't despair; just grate it up and store ready to use in a zip-lock bag. Beeswax has rich emollient properties, which help to protect, soothe, soften and heal the skin. Plus, it's naturally hypoallergenic, great if you have sensitive skin. A word of warning: do not buy cheap beeswax – it just won't have the same properties as the good stuff. If in doubt, Neal's Yard should be your go-to supplier.

BUTTERS

Not the eating kind, but rather plant-based butters used to bind ingredients together. The most popular are cocoa butter and shea butter. Both are widely available and have intensely moisturizing and healing effects on dry skin; they can even, in some cases, be helpful for eczema sufferers. If you fancy using something more exotic, try extra-virgin coconut butter or even Monoi de Tahiti butter, which is made from gardenia blossoms soaked in pure natural coconut butter and smells heavenly.

CARRIER OILS

Essential to most homemade beauty and skin products, carrier oils, as their name suggests, are used primarily to carry diluted essential oils on to the skin and to make fragrant blended massage and facial oils. The most widely used carrier oils are almond, coconut, jojoba, avocado, apricot kernel and wheatgerm. Give these a whirl, or if you feel like splashing out, get your hands on some rosehip or vitamin E oil – both are renowned for their intensive healing and nourishing properties and are excellent in face creams. They can be quite expensive, but you only ever need to use a drop or two in each batch of cream so they will last you a good while.

ESSENTIAL OILS

Essential oils have been used for centuries and have therapeutic properties that can improve both physical and emotional wellbeing. Made from a variety of distilled aromatic plants, flowers and herbs, the oils can be either diluted and absorbed through the pores of the skin or inhaled. You probably already have your tried-and-tested favourites, but if you're not familiar with essential oils, find a health store or chemist that will let you try the scents before you buy. I love heady oriental scents like jasmine, ylang-ylang and neroli, and, of course, nothing beats a lavender bath when you're feeling tired and stressed out.

FRAGRANCE OILS

Blended synthetic oils are used to perfume cosmetics. They aren't natural so they don't have any therapeutic properties, and some people prefer to forgo them completely and stick with essential oils. But if you're anything like me and can't resist the sweet aromas of chocolate and vanilla (generally only available in this form), invest in some fragrance oils to make up luscious lip balms and sweetly scented body lotions or bath bombs. Try to buy the best quality you can afford and always check the manufacturer's guidelines before use, as some may not be suitable for skin application.

FLOWER WATERS

You can use delicately scented floral waters either on their own, for toning the skin, or blended with essential oils, to create refreshing facial mist sprays. They are also effective ingredients in face masks and body lotions. Just pick one to suit your mood!

Remember: Essential oils are extremely concentrated, so you only need a few drops at a time. Never apply undiluted oils directly on to your skin and never drink them! Always read the label – some oils might not be suitable if you're pregnant or have very sensitive skin.

- ◆ Orange flower water
  relaxing and balancing
- ◆ Rose water
  stress-relieving
- ◆ Lavender water
  soothing and calming
- ◆ Peppermint water
  stimulating and energizing
- ◆ Chamomile water
  calming (good for those with fragile or irritated skin)
- ◆ Witch hazel
  astringent and toning

Remember: Make up your homemade natural beauty and skincare products in small batches – you won't be adding preservatives into the mix, so they won't have as long a shelf life as commercially produced products.

• HEAVEN SCENT •

Geranium
balancing and uplifting

Grapefruit
stimulating and refreshing

Jasmine
sensual and aphrodisiac

Lavender
relaxing and healing

Neroli
soothing and restorative

Peppermint
purifying and stimulating

Rose
calming and cleansing

Rosewood
uplifting and aphrodisiac

Sandalwood
warming and aphrodisiac

Tea Tree
antiseptic and uplifting

Ylang-ylang
soothing and relaxing

There are no hard-and-fast rules when it comes to blending essential oils – just follow your nose and mix them to suit your mood. Here are my favourite combinations:

Floral – lavender, rose, jasmine, geranium (florals blend well with woody, citrus or oriental aromas)

Woody – rosewood, sandalwood (woody aromas blend well with most others)

Citrus – grapefruit, neroli (citrus blends well with oriental, minty and floral aromas)

Oriental – jasmine, neroli, ylang-ylang (orientals blend well with floral or citrus aromas)

Medicinal – tea tree (only works well on its own)

Minty – peppermint (minty aromas blend well with citrus and woody scents)

EQUIPMENT

MIXING BOWL

FUNNEL

CONTAINERS

BLENDER OR
FOOD PROCESSOR

MEASURING SPOONS

RUBBER GLOVES
(OPTIONAL)

STIRRERS

SILICONE MOULDS

EQUIPMENT

Really, you hardly need any specialist equipment to make your own beauty products. But there are one or two things you should have to hand (with any luck, most of it should already be in your household kit).

MIXING BOWL
A small microwave-safe glass bowl or a measuring jug would be ideal.

MEASURING SPOONS
It's worth investing in a set of measuring spoons to ensure your tablespoon and teaspoon measures are accurate.

STIRRERS
Now, I say stirrers because the mixtures can often be very greasy and gloopy – you might want something you can dispose of after using. I like to use wooden coffee stirrers (next time you're in Starbucks or Costa, grab a handful!); alternatively, you can buy very cheap wooden lollipop sticks in packs from most good craft shops. A small whisk or a silicone spatula may also be useful for blending ingredients together.

BLENDER OR FOOD PROCESSOR
For grinding up oats and almonds to make face and body scrubs.

COOKING EQUIPMENT
Some of the ingredients in the following recipes will have to be melted down to be blended. Microwaves are handy for making up quick recipes for lip balms and glosses and anything that has only one or two ingredients, but for moisturizers, body balms or soaps it will be better to melt the ingredients gradually on the hob, in a bowl suspended over a pan of simmering water.

FUNNEL
A standard kitchen funnel will do for transferring your homemade oils and lotions to their containers. If you've already been kicking out the jams (see 'Preserving', p. 130), double up and make use of your jam funnel here too.

SILICONE MOULDS
Silicone ice cube trays or chocolate or cupcake moulds are perfect for making bath bombs.

CONTAINERS
Depending on what you decide to make, you will need a selection of containers, including jars, pots, bottles and atomizers. Either buy empty travel containers from a pharmacy (and Muji stock a good range) or recycle the old containers of shop-bought beauty products. Mini jam jars also make the most adorable containers for your homemade potions. Just make sure you thoroughly clean them before reusing. And don't forget to make cute hand-drawn labels (see p. 149).

RUBBER GLOVES (OPTIONAL)
If you have sensitive skin, wear rubber or latex gloves when handling concentrated oils or spices to prevent any irritation from spillages.

Now you've been read the DIY beauty riot act and you're armed with a list of naturally nourishing ingredients, without further ado here are some of my tried-and-tested recipes for you to try. Feel free to get experimental and customize to suit your own needs. Generally, most of the butters, carrier oils and essential oils can be switched around, according to what you have to hand or to suit your personal preferences. Write down any recipe alterations to use when you want to recreate your own signature blends.

Caution: Make sure you are not allergic to any of the ingredients before you use them.

DIY SPARKLES

Let's start as we mean to go on and kick things off with a little Ziggy Stardust.

Keep a selection of fine loose cosmetic glitter in your stash (Claire's Accessories sell it in rainbow-hued stacking pots) to pick and mix to match your outfit. You will also need aloe vera gel, which you can pick up from Holland and Barrett – just make sure you buy colourless, as green will interfere with your customized colours. Use your fingers or a make-up brush to smudge around your eyes (not in your eyes!) or smear all over your body to be a real disco dolly. At the end of the night, remove with warm water and a washcloth.

You will need:

• 30ml pot
• Aloe vera gel
• 1 tsp loose very fine glitter
• 1 drop of essential oil (optional)

Making:

1. Squeeze as much aloe vera gel as you can into your container.

2. Add 1 tsp of the loose glitter and blend with a stirrer.

3. If using, add 1–2 drops of essential oil. I like lavender or ylang-ylang – both smell sweet but are not too overwhelming.

KEEP IT TIDY!

To keep your mixing bowls and apparatus clean and gloop free (some of the melted ingredients can get sticky and leave thick waxy residues once cooled), simply wipe down before they dry with a cloth or paper towel, then wash as normal with hot soapy water.

KEEP IT CLEAN!

Make sure your hands and all your equipment, including your containers, are thoroughly clean before you start, to prevent bacteria spreading and to ensure your homemade lotions and potions will last as long as possible.

LUSCIOUS LIPS

Everyone wants a pouting pair
of luscious lips, so do your lips
a service and whip up your own
deliciously edible homemade balms
and glosses. They beat shop-bought
versions hands down and make
perfect presents to boot.

Here's a tip: use a toothbrush to
exfoliate your lips several times a week.
An old schoolfriend taught me this trick
– she even used to mix up a mini lip
scrub made from 1 tsp granulated sugar,
a squirt of honey and a drop of jojoba or
Vitamin E oil, both of which are super
duper for solving any unsightly lip
soreness. Apply to your lips with
fingertips and exfoliate gently before
washing off with warm water.

GET LIPPY LIP BALM

Now, you can make a quick lippy fix by simply mixing some Vaseline with a bit of old lipstick and a drop of essential oil, but if you have the time, this gorgeous lip balm made entirely from scratch is well worth the effort. Thick, luxurious and deliciously moisturizing, it can be kept simple or tinted by adding a chunk of lipstick. You can even boost its aroma by adding a couple of drops of your favourite essential oil, if you like.

You will need:

- 30ml container
- 2 tsp beeswax
- 2 tsp coconut oil – from the cooking section of the supermarket or health food shop
- 1 tsp vitamin E oil
- 1 tsp vanilla oil or extract
- An old lipstick to tint (optional)

Making:

1. In a bowl placed over a saucepan of simmering water, heat the beeswax and coconut oil, stirring regularly until fully melted.

2. Leave to cool for 5 minutes, then stir in the vitamin E oil, vanilla oil or extract and lipstick if using (you may need to blend with the back of a spoon).

3. Pour the mixture into a clean container and leave in the fridge for 30 minutes before using.

LIPS LIKE SUGAR GLOSS

Give your lips a glossy sheen with this sweet tinted lip-gloss. No need to add flavouring – the honey will be sweet enough and will also give your lips a natural gloss. A touch of edible glitter will be a deliciously sparkly addition – buy from a cookware shop or make your own (see p. 125). Just remember to make it very fine as you want to add a light dust of shimmer not pop rocks of powder.

Making:

1. In a bowl placed over a saucepan of simmering water, heat the coconut butter, stirring regularly until fully melted, then set aside to cool.

2. In a separate bowl, use the back of a spoon to blend the Vaseline and a couple of centimetres of the lipstick until fully incorporated. Pour in the butter, add the honey and blend again.

3. Finally, stir in the glitter (if using), then pour the mixture into the container and place in the freezer for 10–15 minutes before using.

You will need:

- 30ml container
- 1 tbsp coconut butter
- 2 tbsp Vaseline
- An old lipstick
- 1 tsp clear honey
- 1 tsp edible glitter (optional)

✗ ✗ ✗

TONERS

Toning is an important part of any girl's beauty regime and you may be surprised just how effective some simple kitchen ingredients can be for the job. To use, moisten some cotton wool with your toner, then pat on to the skin and leave to dry. And ladies, avoid direct contact with your eyes. If you know your skin is easily irritated, do a patch test (see opposite) before using on your face.

CLEANSING TONER

Cider vinegar is great for cleansing and tightening the skin's pores, as well as for clearing up unsightly blemishes. The rose water (which you can also buy from the supermarket) adds a gorgeous aroma and helps to soothe irritated skin.

You will need:

- 100ml bottle
- 6 tbsp purified water
- 1 tbsp cider vinegar
- 2 tbsp rose water

Making:

1. Pour the water and cider vinegar into the bottle, close the lid and shake until fully combined.

2. Add the rose water and give it another shake.

ORANGE FLOWER TONER

You will need:

- 100ml bottle
- 3 tbsp purified water
- 3 tbsp witch hazel
- 3 tbsp orange flower water
- 1 drop of lavender essential oil

Witch hazel, which you can buy from the chemist, is a natural astringent, great for blemishes. (The Native Americans were early discoverers of its healing properties and used it for a whole range of medicinal purposes.) The orange flower water (buy from the supermarket) helps smooth and refine uneven skin. The perfect refreshing toner for stuffy aeroplane journeys.

Making:

1. Pour the purified water and the witch hazel into the bottle, close the lid and shake until fully combined.

2. Add the orange flower water and the lavender oil and give it another shake.

PATCH TEST

If you have sensitive skin, make sure you patch test your homemade creams and lotions before you use them. The best place to test is on the delicate skin on the inside of your wrist, so dab a bit of whatever you are testing on to your pulse point, then leave for 24 hours. If you spot any signs of irritation – a rash, excessive redness, itching, pain or flaking skin – then wash off immediately and if symptoms persist, see a doctor. If you have no reaction, it will be safe to use the product as normal.

FACE MASKS AND SCRUBS

Sometimes your face needs a little extra TLC and what better way to give it than with a cleansing face mask or a revitalizing facial scrub?

RELAXING ROSE CLAY MASK

White clay, which you can buy online (see 'Address Book', p.235), is extremely gentle on the skin and can help stimulate the circulation and extract impurities. It is also wonderfully soothing, perfect for dry or sensitive skin. Rosehip oil is intensely nourishing – although it can be expensive, a small bottle will last you a long time. Make up this mask as and when you need it.

You will need:

- 2 tbsp white clay
- 3 tbsp rose water
- 1 tsp rosehip oil

Making:

1. In a bowl, mix the clay with the rose water until you have a smooth paste.

2. Stir in the rosehip oil.

To use:

Tie your hair back and, using your fingertips, apply the mask directly on to clean skin, leaving little panda rings from the top of your eyebrows to directly beneath your eyes. Then sit back, relax and let the mask do its thing for 15 minutes before washing off with a washcloth and some warm water.

Finish off with some moisturizer to keep your skin soft and supple. Use once a week.

BE
YOUR
OWN
BEAUTY
EXPERT

HOMEMADE
HONEY ALMOND & OAT
FACE SCRUB
EST. 2011

ALMOND, OAT AND
HONEY FACE SCRUB

The ground oats and almonds (which you can buy from the supermarket) in this delectable scrub subtly exfoliate, helping to brighten and lift your complexion. Honey is a natural moisturizer, which will leave your skin feeling smooth and silky soft. Keep in the fridge between applications.

You will need:

- 100ml jar
- 1 tbsp ground almonds
- 1 tbsp ground uncooked oats
- 5 drops of vitamin E oil
- 1 tsp clear honey
- Drop of water

Making:

1. In a bowl, combine the ground almonds and oats.

2. Add the vitamin E oil, stir in the honey and a drop of water to loosen before mixing until thoroughly combined.

To use:

Always use your face scrub after toning and be gentle – you don't want to aggravate your skin and make it red and angry. Use your fingertips to gently rub the scrub into your face using small circular motions, which should leave your skin feeling polished and give you back your glow, before washing off with a wash-cloth and some warm water. Use once a week.

MOISTURIZERS
AND OILS

A good moisturizer should be both nourishing and hydrating and should lubricate as well as smooth the skin.

Most of us like to use moisturizer at least once, if not twice, a day, which can make it a very expensive habit. So save some pennies and make up your own, scented with your favourite aromas. Apply to warm damp skin and use your fingertips to massage into the face using small circular upwards motions.

Body oils are also great for soft and supple skin, and are best applied after exfoliation (see p. 191) to warm damp skin, ideally after a hot bath. Massage into the skin before blotting with a dry towel to remove any excess.

FEED YOUR FACE MOISTURIZER

Works beautifully for both night and day. Just blend essential oils to suit your mood: for an uplifting day cream, use a mix of ylang-ylang and neroli, or for a soothing night-time treat, try lavender and geranium.

You will need:

- 60ml container
- 1 tbsp beeswax
- 6 tbsp almond oil
- 1 tbsp orange flower water
- 3 drops of essential oil

Making:

1. In a bowl placed over a saucepan of simmering water, heat the beeswax, stirring regularly until fully melted. Remove from the heat and leave to cool for 5 minutes before stirring in the almond oil. As the mixture cools, it will thicken and become milky in colour.

2. Add the orange flower water and the essential oil and stir. After one final mix, spoon into your container. Cool in the fridge for 30 minutes before using.

HEAVENLY HAND CREAM

This soothing hand cream will help heal dry, cracked and over-worked hands. Make in a small container to keep in your handbag.

You will need:

- 60ml container
- ½ tbsp beeswax
- ½ tbsp shea butter
- 1 tbsp almond oil
- 1 tbsp apricot kernel oil
- 2 tbsp rose water
- ½ tbsp aloe vera gel

Making:

1. In a bowl placed over a saucepan of simmering water, heat the beeswax and shea butter, stirring regularly until fully melted. Remove from the heat and leave to cool before stirring in the oils.

2. Add the rose water, and finally the aloe vera gel. Stir to combine.

3. Pour into the container and leave to cool in the fridge for 30 minutes before using.

RICH VANILLA BODY OIL

This rich body oil smells simply divine, and you can use it on your face, your body and even your hair. (The lotion will go hard in cold weather and more oil-like in warm weather.) Perfect for post-beach pampering. I can't get enough of this stuff when I'm on holiday, and once you've tried it, neither will you!

You will need:

- 100ml container
- 2 tbsp coconut butter
- 2 tbsp coconut oil – from the cooking section of the supermarket or health food shop
- 1 tsp clear honey
- 4 tbsp almond oil
- 1 tsp vanilla oil

Making:

1. In a bowl placed over a saucepan of simmering water, heat the coconut butter, stirring regularly until fully melted.

2. Add the coconut oil and honey, stir until thoroughly combined and then remove from the heat and let cool slightly.

3. Stir in the almond oil, then mix in the vanilla oil and stir again. Pour into the container and leave for 30 minutes at room temperature before using.

BATH-TIME TREATS

Keep your body beautiful with some luxuriously scented salt and sugar scrubs – getting into the habit of exfoliating will give you silky-soft skin. I used to spend vast amounts of money on expensive scrubs until I found out how easy it was to make my own. Just mix nourishing oils with therapeutic salts, like Epsom, for a spa experience on a shoestring budget. These make the most perfect gifts – you can personalize the scents to suit your friends.

SALT BODY SCRUB

This is my go-to body scrub recipe, as it's just so easy to customize. Try mixing it up by switching the carrier oil – jojoba, avocado and apricot kernel oil will all work well. Then pick an essential oil to suit – rose, geranium, peppermint, lavender, grapefruit, whatever tickles your fancy. Salt scrubs are best used on damp skin, so use once or twice a week in the bath or the shower – just make sure you don't get any water in the scrub, which will spoil its magic. If you don't have specialist cup measures, use a teacup to measure the salts and almond oil.

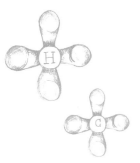

You will need:

- Medium-sized jar (a small Kilner jar is perfect)
- 1 cup Epsom salts
- 1 cup sea salt
- 2 cups almond oil
- 6 drops of essential oils

Making:

1. In a bowl, combine the Epsom salts and the sea salt.

2. Stir in the almond oil. Don't worry if the salts and the oil separate – this is natural and won't affect your use of the scrub. Then add the essential oil and stir again.

3. Transfer the mixture to your container.

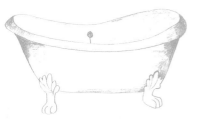

PEPPERMINT FOOT SCRUB

A foot bath is a real treat – made even better if you can get a bunch of friends together and have a spa party (see right for more ideas for pamper parties). Peppermint is not only invigorating but also has potent healing properties and can give you a real energy boost at the end of a hard day's work. The Epsom salts help to detoxify and exfoliate the skin, while the mineral-rich Pink Himalaya bath salts, which you can buy from the chemist, will make your scrub pretty in pink.

You will need:

- Small jar
- 2 tbsp Dead Sea salts
- 2 tbsp Epsom salts
- 4 tbsp Pink Himalaya bath salts
- 4 tbsp almond oil
- 6 drops of peppermint essential oil

Making:

1. In a bowl, combine the Epsom and Dead Sea salts and the Pink Himalaya bath salts.

2. Gradually add in the almond oil, stirring to combine. Add the peppermint essential oil and stir again.

3. Transfer to your container.

To use:

Soak your feet in hot water for 5–10 minutes, then towel dry. Massage the scrub into your feet, taking care on the sensitive parts and making sure you give your heels a good scrubbing. Rinse off and towel dry. Now put your feet up and relax!

FIZZY BATH BOMBS

Bath bombs are effervescent bath soaps that bubble up into a fragrant fizz when dropped into water. They make brilliant presents as they can be set into shapes using fun moulds.

Warning: You must keep all your equipment, including your hands, absolutely dry. The ingredients are extremely reactive and any moisture could dampen the bath bombs' overall fizzability!

You will need:

- 4 tbsp bicarbonate of soda
- 2 tbsp citric acid – from the supermarket baking aisle
- A sprinkling of dried flowers
- 1 tbsp almond oil
- 1–2 drops of food colouring
- 10 drops of essential oil
- Witch hazel in a spray bottle
- Silicone moulds
- Foil

Making:

1. In a dry glass bowl, mix together the bicarbonate of soda and the citric acid. Make sure they are completely combined before attempting the next stage. If I have time, I sift the mixture a few times to make sure. (If these ingredients are not mixed properly, the bomb will be grainy in texture.)

2. Stir in the dried flowers. Add the almond oil, a drop or two of food colouring and the essential oil and mix well.

3. The next step is a little tricky – your bomb is going to start fizzing as soon as you add the witch hazel, so you will have to work fast. Start spritzing the mixture with the witch hazel, a little at a time – you don't want to get the mixture too wet. Continue to stir as you do this until the mixture is crumbly but will form in your hand.

4. Now pack the mixture tightly into the moulds. Keep pressing it down – you want to get as much of the mixture as you can into each mould. Leave overnight in a warm dry place, away from any moisture or direct sunlight.

5. Next day, carefully remove the bombs from the moulds and wrap in foil, which will protect them from moisture. For best results, use immediately or within 1 to 2 weeks – the longer you keep them, the less fizzy they will be.

WITH A LITTLE HELP FROM YOUR FRIENDS – HOST A PAMPER PARTY

So now you've got some delicious recipes to try out, get the girls round for a pamper party. Everyone deserves a bit of a pampering now and then and, while spas are too pricey for most, you needn't miss out – it's so easy and buckets of fun to host your own DIY spa day.

Hen parties and birthdays are the perfect excuse to try home facials, swap your homemade lotions and take turns to give each other mini manicures, pedicures, face masks and foot baths, as well as share beauty secrets.

Set the date, write your invites and ask your guests to bring along their beauty essentials: nail varnishes, manicure kits, cotton pads, bathrobes. It can also be a good idea to pool resources to cover the cost of ingredients – ask each guest to bring along something that can be shared among the group. Set up seating areas and create a relaxing atmosphere with some music and scented candles. And don't forget to offer some light food and refreshments– try some delicately delicious herbal tea infusions (see p. 166). Work out a schedule for treatments so your guests can take it in turns to give each other foot soaks and massages. Or set up a make-up station and get busy mixing up glitter gels, tinted balms and bath bombs. Or just slap on some beauty masks and catch up on some girlie gossip.

2m Super-Elastic

2m Standard-Elastic

LAST
ONE
99p

MAKE DO
AND
MEND

Make Do and Mend

The Make Do and Mend philosophy has been given the kiss of life in recent years and has come smack back into fashion with a thoroughly modern mission. A new generation, eager to recycle, reuse and revamp, are embracing the thrifty, resourceful approach to life of 70 years ago. As landfills overflow with rubbish, climate change accelerates and spending habits are reviewed, there's never been a better time to look to the frugal ways of the 30s and 40s. So whether you want to make do and mend your home or your wardrobe, or simply learn a few time-honoured tricks, look no further — I will show you how to mend it with style! Don't feel daunted — all the following tips and techniques require only the simplest of hand-sewing skills, all of which are fully explained in 'Stitchcraft' (p. 52). And between you and me, a little dab of fabric glue here and there never hurt. Just saying . . .

> ## Nostalgia ain't
> ## what it used to be

During the war years, the Make Do and Mend movement played an important role in the life of everyone in Britain. The country was warned to beware of the squander bug as people were encouraged to salvage everything. A shortage of raw materials and lack of factory space (as manufacturers gave priority to making uniforms) eventually led to clothes rationing, so women had to learn how to make do with what they already had.

Posters and pamphlets featuring 'Mrs Sew and Sew' offered practical advice on how to make clothes last as long as possible. (Some of this vintage advice is being reissued today.) In response, our fashionista forebears invented cast-off couture and became masterminds of the makeover. My great-granny Dolly was one such woman – she used to hand sew all my grandmother's clothes, spending her evenings knocking up outfits out of all sorts of oddments, like old curtains and worn-out cushion covers.

Rationing meant that women were allowed to buy only one outfit a year. Can you imagine! So to keep their threads fresh, women had to get creative and revamp old favourites in all sorts of weird and wonderful ways – shoes were made from cork, hats from newspaper, and black-out blinds became new frocks. Cosmetics were hard to come by and old lipsticks were melted down and repotted. Even stockings became black-market contraband, and they were so scarce that many women had to resort to browning their legs with gravy and applying a streak of eye pencil for a mock seam. And if ladies needed new underwear, well, they had to make it themselves, unpicking and reknitting worn-out woollies.

Today the Make Do and Mend ethos is being revived by the emerging DIY fashion movement. Restyling clothes is all the rage, and more and more people are empowering themselves through their ability to recreate rather than their ability to shop. And being inventive with how you refashion clothes is all part of the fun of creating something new out of something old. So when you put your skills to the test, try to improvise, work with what you've already got and resist the urge to splurge. Check out my DIY fashion tips on pp. 207–9 to learn some cheap tricks to create new looks and save some pennies too.

Fix Up, Look Sharp – Mend Your Ways with These Simple Hand-Sewing Repair Skills

A stitch in time really does save nine and learning how to mend your clothes will keep them looking their best for longer. You'll need minimal hand-sewing skills, so once you've mastered the basics, it's just a matter of getting into the habit of fixing things before they go beyond the point of no repair. Nobody likes to say goodbye to a well-loved item of clothing – long before I started mending my clothes, my mum used to call me 'Orphan Annie', as I'd wander about in my most prized vintage attire all torn and tattered, hems hanging loose and rips on every seam, looking as if I'd just stepped out of a nineteenth-century workhouse. Thankfully, these days I know my French seams from my French tucks since my granny made it her mission to teach me all that she knew.

Make your mending more merry and hold a Make Do and Mend party, and while you're at it, why not organize a stash exchange to swap stockpiles of fabrics, buttons and any other crafty bits and bobs? (See p. 214 for more gatherings ideas.) Now, needles at the ready – you'll soon see how just a few simple skills will have you fixed up and looking sharp in no time.

HOW TO SEW ON A BUTTON

I've lost count of the number of times people have asked me to do this for them – c'mon, guys, it's easy! You can use normal sewing thread for attaching buttons to lightweight fabrics, but for things like coats, trousers and jackets, which are made from heavier fabrics, use a special buttonhole twist (a more robust thread) to keep things secure for longer. The general method of button basting will depend on what sort of button you want to affix: a flat two-hole, a four-hole or a shank.

FLAT BUTTONS

These are your classic two-hole or four-hole buttons. To sew a flat button down, thread up a needle with a long length of matching thread, then knot the end (remembering to use double thread for heavy fabrics). Placing the button precisely will make all the difference, so have a good look on your garment for the position of the missing button. Once you've found it, bring the tip of the needle through the back of the garment and make a couple of fix stitches (see p. 62) to anchor the thread. Holding the

button down with your fingers, bring the tip of the needle through the holes of the button, then bring it back down; repeat several times until you have a sturdy fix. If you are attaching a two-hole button, stitch up through one hole and down through the other. For a four-hole button, you can sew through the holes in a variety of ways: parallel lines, as a cross, in a square or even as an arrow. Or for a bit of fun, why not use contrasting thread for a decorative finish? Finally, to fasten off, bring the needle to the front of the work and wrap the thread around the stitches behind the button about 3 or 4 times before bringing the needle to the back of the fabric and securing with a few fix stitches. Cut the thread close to the stitches.

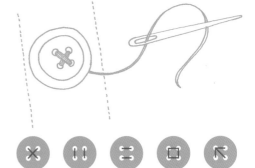

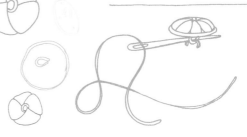

SHANK BUTTONS

Shanks are a particular type of decorative button used mainly on jackets and coats. They have a raised button head with a thread shank (small ring) on the underside that allows extra space for the fabric around the buttonhole to sit between the button and the garment. First, decide where you want to attach the shank and mark the position with tailor's chalk. Double-thread the needle (see my basic needle-threading tips on p. 63) and tie a knot in the end of the thread. Bring the tip of the needle through the back of the garment to make a few fix stitches (see p. 62) to anchor the thread. Next, bring the needle up through the fabric and through the button shank itself (keeping the button head angled down with your other hand) then bring it back down through the fabric. Pass the needle back and forth like this a few times, keeping the stitches parallel and taut (but not too tight or the button will sink into the fabric). Then bring the needle to the front and wrap the thread around the stitches holding the shank to the fabric about three or four times before bringing the needle back behind the fabric to fasten off. Make a couple of fix stitches, then tie a knot in the thread, pull it tight and cut the thread off close to the knot.

✳✳✳✳✳✳ BUTTON TIP ✳✳✳✳✳✳

Always keep the extra buttons you get given with brand-new clothes in a separate box to your other button booty. That way, when you need to find a particular one, you won't have to spend too much time rummaging around for it.

✳✳✳✳✳✳✳✳✳✳✳✳✳✳✳✳✳✳✳✳✳✳✳✳

CUTE AS A BUTTON – HOW TO COVER BUTTONS

Prettying up your buttons by covering them with your favourite fabrics is easy-peasy. Make them to match an outfit, or use clashing colours and prints to add some contrasting decorative detail. You can either use a pre-existing shank button or buy some plastic self-cover buttons (white plastic buttons with snap-on shanks) in your preferred size from a haberdashery store. Then measure the diameter of the button head and cut out a circle of fabric double that size – the material should be twice the circumference of the button head. Then sew a running stitch (see p. 61) around the edge of the material, leave the needle attached and gather up the stitches by carefully pulling the thread to tighten it around and behind the button head. Rearrange the gathers using your needle if necessary, until the front and the back of the button look neat. If you are using a normal shank button, slip the needle through the stitches a few times to secure, then knot and cut the thread. Or if you are using self-cover buttons, first knot the thread, then snap the button shank on to the back. Easy!

HOW TO FIX A HEM

Nothing is more irritating than a loose hem, and they always seem to catch when you're out and about having fun without a needle to hand. Iron-on fusible webbing tape or even a dab of fabric glue will provide a fast fix, but if a job is worth doing, it's worth doing properly.

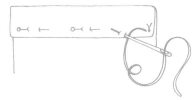

All you need to keep your hems hanging high are a few simple slipstitches. Start by turning the garment inside out and surveying the damage. If a large length of the hem has come undone, press it back into place with an iron, with the raw edge turned under to its original position, before pinning down. If it's only a small repair, simply press down with your fingers before pinning into place. Now, you'll want your hem to be invisible from the right side. First thread up a needle with some matching thread – single thread for a light material, double thread for heavier fabric. Then insert the needle inside the turned edge and pick up only one or two thread fibres, just enough to hold the two pieces of fabric together, and begin to work a slipstitch (see p. 62) diagonally from right to left. When you come to the end, sew a small fix stitch to keep in place.

Put a Patch On It

Knowing how to patch up holes and tears is a handy trick to have up your sleeve – and patches can be decorative as well as functional. Jeans with patches may sound super retro, but in fact they look super cute. Pick a contrasting fabric like floral chintz cotton for a cheery decorative detail and add on to the knee or the back of a pair of jeans. Or why not attach some granddad patches to your jacket or sweater using scrap suede or leather?

HOW TO FIX A RIPPED SEAM

Wear and tear is part of everyday life and ripped seams are a common problem. But they can easily be fixed if you catch them early.

If the fabric around the ripped seam is still intact, simply snip away any straggly threads and press the seam down to neaten before you stitch. Place the two seam edges together, right sides facing, then, following the original seam line, sew either by hand using a backstitch (see p. 61), anchoring with a fix stitch (p. 62) and a small knot at either end, or on the machine using a running stitch.

Consider reinforcing the seam to prevent further splitting. Place a fabric scrap (a small length of ribbon or bias tape would also do) over some iron-on fusible webbing on top of the underside of the seam. Iron on (make sure you read the manufacturer's guidelines first) and secure with a backstitch too.

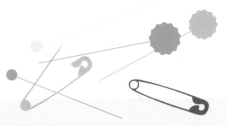

Start by trimming the tear you want to mend into a neat square or rectangle, then snip a notch (about 6 mm) into each corner of the cut-out shape. Turn the garment inside out to press these 6 mm edges flat on to the wrong side of the fabric. Next, cut out a patch from your chosen fabric about 1 cm larger on all sides than the hole. Place the patch on top of the hole with the right side of the patch facing out and pin into place from behind. Turn the garment right side out and slipstitch (see p. 62) the patch into place around the edges. Then turn inside out again, remove the pins, trim the edges of the patch and you're done.

Sweet Vintage Dreams

My love for vintage doesn't stop at clothing — oh no. In fact, my craze for kitsch carries on right through the house and into the bedroom. Some of my favourite finds in flea markets and second-hand shops are retro linens and bed sheets. Vintage floral, soft paisley, colourful 60s prints and 70s swirls; if only bed linens nowadays were as groovy. When treasure-hunting for bed linens, steer clear of polyester and nylon, which don't absorb moisture so can lead to a sweaty night's sleep, and they won't be as cosy to cuddle up in. My mum is positively squeamish when it comes to synthetic fabrics, almost to the point of phobia. She once kicked a friend out of bed at a schoolgirl slumber party for having the audacity to sleep next to her wearing a nylon nightie. Simply by association, I too have become a dab hand at telling the difference between natural and man-made. The best way is to get up close and personal and have a good feel. Polyester usually has a slippery sheen to it.

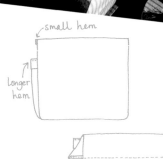

Peace-Out Pillowcase

Vintage sheets, unfortunately, tend to be worn and faded in parts but rather than leaving them to pale into obscurity, I like to cut them up to restyle them, usually adding a pink cotton lace trim or some decorative ribbon. Have a go at making your perfect pillowcase. Just make sure you wash and iron your vintage sheet before you begin.

YOU WILL NEED:
- 1 cotton bed sheet (for cutting up)
- Lace, satin ribbon or appliqué trimmings
- Matching threads
- Fabric scissors
- Pins
- Measuring tape
- Fabric marking pen
- Sewing machine
- Iron

* * * * * *

Makes a standard-sized rectangular pillowcase (75 cm x 50 cm)

* * * * * *

MAKING:

1. Lay the sheet out flat and check for any damage so you know where to avoid when marking and cutting. On the wrong side of the fabric, measure, mark with your fabric pen and cut out a 166 x 51 cm rectangle (this includes seam allowances).

2. First hem both of the shorter ends of your fabric rectangle. One end of the pillowcase will have an 8 cm hem, and the other end will have a smaller 2 cm turning. Begin with the smaller hem first: with the wrong side of the fabric facing you, turn a 2 cm hem down on to the wrong side of the fabric, press with an iron and then sew on the machine using a straight stitch (see p. 76).

3. Now hem the opposite end. Again, with the wrong side of the fabric facing you, turn a 1 cm hem down, press with an iron, then fold over another 7 cm and press again. Sew this hem down close to the edge on the machine with a straight stitch.

4. Next, add your decorative trims. Lay your rectangle out with the smallest hem at the top. With the right side of the fabric facing you, measure 25 cm from the top edge and pin your decorative trim in a long strip across the width of the pillowcase. Sew into place.

5. Keeping your rectangle with the smaller hem at the top and the right side of the fabric facing you, fold to bring the edge of the bigger hem 18 cm from the top of the smaller hem. Press and pin the two sides together.

6. To make the envelope flap that will keep the pillow encased, fold 12 cm of the end with the smaller hem over to the wrong side of the fabric. Pin along the two sides and sew 6 mm from the edge along the whole of both sides.

7. Snip the four corners diagonally to get rid of excess material. Turn the pillowcase right side out, then work out the corners. Press, and you're done!

small hem

longer hem

Small hem

DIY DOILY IDEAS

Oh doily, how do I love thee? Let me count the ways. I could find a hundred uses for the darling but defunct doily. Most people either love 'em or hate 'em but whether you're a doily enthusiast or a doily detester, I'm going to share my mad love for the holey one in a celebration of all things granny chic. They can be picked up for literally pennies at any charity shop, garage sale or second-hand market and there is never any shortage of supply. You may even be lucky enough to have a kindly elderly relative willing to donate a stash of them. In which case, there's no excuse not to DIY with your doilies . . .

DOILY CUSHION COVER

Find a doily that delights and use it to dress up a boring cushion cover. A plain ready-made cover will do (if you don't have one at home already, pick one up at Ikea), or go the whole hog and sew your own. Then simply stitch the doily to the front of the cushion by hand with a whipstitch (see p. 61) or use the machine to topstitch in place. Go one step further and dye your doily to match or contrast with the cushion cover (dye in a stainless steel sink or a bucket dye bath, making sure you follow the manufacturer's guidelines). Or try stitching a number of doilies together edge to edge with a whipstitch to build up a larger design before attaching in one large piece on to the front or back (or both) of your cushion.

DOILY TABLE RUNNER

Collect a diversity of doilies, then dye them in a rainbow of colours (or keep it simple with one shade, or even leave them undyed) before stitching them together edge to edge with some heavy thread and a whipstitch (see p. 61) to create either a long table runner or a tablecloth.

Curtain Call — Tea Cloth Tab-Top Curtains

Over the years, I have amassed a cupboard-busting collection of vintage tea cloths, and I recently put them to good use in a pair of these adorable tab-top curtains. Vintage lace, napkins, tea cloths and handkerchiefs can be picked up dime a dozen; sew them against a pair of tab-top curtains and you'll be displaying a century's worth of handiwork on your curtain pole in no time.

BEFORE YOU BEGIN:

MEASUREMENTS To work out how big your finished curtain should be (and how much material you will need to make it), either measure an existing curtain or take some measurements from your window. For the length, measure from just beneath your curtain pole to the point where you want your curtains to stop (do you want them to go to the floor or just to the windowsill?), then add an extra 20 cm to allow for a 10 cm hem top and bottom. For the width, measure the width of your window, multiply by 1.5 if you want a full curtain or leave as it is if you want it to fit exactly, then add 16 cm to allow for an 8 cm seam either side. You will also need extra fabric to make the tabs that hang the curtain to the pole and a strip of facing to attach the tabs to the curtain.

FABRIC Choose a white or pale-coloured medium- to lightweight cotton (an old bed sheet would be ideal). Wash and iron before you begin, to prevent any distortion when you come to wash your curtain for the first time.

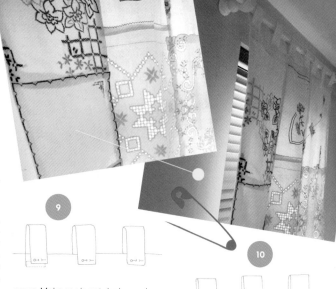

- A selection of small square and rectangular napkins, tea cloths or lace handkerchiefs for the decorative panel
- White cotton fabric to make the curtain and the tab loops
- Matching cotton sewing thread
- Tape measure
- Fabric scissors
- Pins
- Sewing machine

* * * * * *

MAKING:

1. Make the decorative panel. Lay out your collection of napkins, cloths and handkerchiefs and arrange and rearrange them until you find a pleasing combination (overlapping pieces if necessary) that exactly fits your curtain measurements – the outside edge of this decorative panel must line up on all sides with the curtain to give a neat finish.

2. Pin the pieces together before sewing them either with a backstitch or whipstitch (see p. 61) by hand or using a straight stitch on the machine. The best way to do this is to sew them together in long strips, then join the strips together.

3. Make the curtain. Cut out the fabric to the required size, remembering to include 8 cm on either side and 10 cm at the top and bottom for hems.

4. Turn the raw edges over 4 cm on to the wrong side of the fabric on each side of the curtain and press. Then turn another 4 cm down, press again and pin or tack before sewing into place either by hand using a slipstitch (see p. 62) or with a topstitch on the machine. Remove tacking stitches (if you made them) and press.

5. Make the tab loops. Cut a very long length of fabric 12 cm wide. The exact length of this strip will depend on how many tabs you need – you want enough to fit along the width of the curtain with about an 8 cm gap between each tab.

6. Fold the strip in half lengthwise with right sides facing together and

press. Make one long tube by sewing along the length of the strip 6 mm from the cut edges. Turn right side out and press with the seam at one edge.

7. Cut the strip into smaller lengths of identical size, and fold these in half to make your loop tabs. Mine were cut 17 cm long giving a folded size of 8 cm, allowing for a 1 cm seam allowance.

8. Make the facing. Cut out a strip of fabric the same width as your curtain, plus 2 cm (allow for a 1 cm seam allowance on each side) and 10 cm deep. Press a 1 cm hem along one of the long edges.

9. Attach the tab loops. Fold each tab loop in half and pin them about 8 cm apart along the top of the right side of the curtain, with the open edge of the loops at the top.

10. Now place the facing strip right side down on top of the tabs, aligning the turned-under hem with the top of the curtain and the open edges of the tab loops. Pin the three layers together and sew along the top 1 cm from the edge, catching the tab loops in the seam.

11. Pull the facing strip up, over and behind the curtain so that the tab loops now sit on top of the curtain.

press. Tuck the long raw edge of the facing strip under, press and stitch down. Fold over the 1 cm overhang on each side of the facing strip, press and then stitch down as close to the edge as you can.

12. Finish the curtain. Now you need to hem the bottom of the curtain. To make sure you do this in the right place, check the curtain against your window before turning the raw edge under to the wrong side of the fabric, pressing and pinning in place. Sew the bottom hem by hand using a slipstitch (p. 62).

13. Make up. Lay the decorative panel on top of the curtain with right side facing you, aligning the top of the decorative panel with the bottom of the tab loops. Pin into place. Stitch by hand with a slipstitch or topstitch on the machine as close to the edge as you can. Finally, sew the two side seams together.

14. Breathe a sigh of contentment – you now have a beautiful and one-of-a-kind curtain! So thread the pole through the tabs and hang it with pride.

Make Do and Mend Hand Towels

Revamp your bathroom on a budget by giving your torn and tattered hand towels a makeover. Impress your guests when they come to stay with a pretty hand-stitched ribbon trim, appliqué monograms or whatever takes your fancy. These customized towels also make sweet house-warming gifts.

REMOVE TEA STAINS

There's no point crying over spilt milk! Don't be discouraged by discoloured tea stains on old linen or lace – any badly blotched pieces can be soaked in a bucket of warm water with some strong detergent and a splash of bleach. Leave overnight before rinsing out and washing and drying as normal. If the stains don't lift, leave them to soak for another 24 hours before rinsing out again.

✶ ✶ ✶ ✶ ✶ ✶
YOU WILL NEED:

• An old bath towel (with a large undamaged area)
• Ribbon or double-fold binding tape for encasing edges, at least 5 cm wide
• Matching thread
• Tape measure
• Fabric scissors
• Pins
• Fabric marker
• Sewing machine
✶ ✶ ✶ ✶ ✶ ✶

MAKING:

1. Lay the towel on a cutting surface and trim away any unsightly frayed edges or ripped areas leaving the largest possible piece. Measure and mark out either a rectangle or a square. You may be able to make two hand towels – cut out the marked shape and fold in half; if it looks large enough, cut along the fold to make a pair.

2. Cut a length of ribbon or double-fold binding tape as long as the sum of the four edges of the towel plus an extra 15 cm for finishing. If using ribbon, fold it in half lengthwise and press with an iron. Then, beginning in the middle of one edge of the towel, position the folded ribbon or binding tape around the edges of the towel, remembering to mitre the corners (see p. 68) as you go, and pin into place. It's best to also tack into place (especially if using ribbon, which can be slippery, making it tricky to sew accurately).

3. Then, either by hand using a slipstitch (see p. 62) or on the machine using a topstitch (see p. 76), sew down close to the edge of the binding making sure to stitch through all three layers as you go. Stop stitching about 2.5 cm before the end of binding, fold the raw edge under 1 cm and stitch to the end.

4. Finally, attach any appliqué designs by sewing around the edges with a slipstitch or topstitch on the machine.

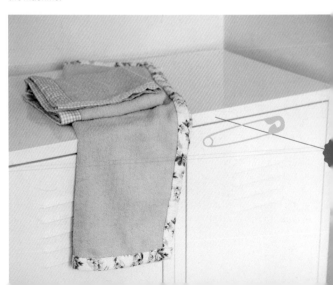

DIY Fashion

Do-it-yourself fashion is perfect for the conscientious girl in need of a quick fashion fix. Concerns about the effects of fast fashion and sweat shop labour conditions have seen the development of an ethical fashion movement. People are now questioning where and how their clothes are made and at what cost. Plus, as any dedicated follower of fashion knows, splurging on new gear from season to season can be expensive. So follow the DIY fashion challenge, unleash your creative streak and come up with innovative ways to revitalize last season's cast-offs into this season's must-haves.

Haberdashery Heaven

Customizing clothes using decorative sewing techniques and embellishments is an easy way to add detail and attitude to outmoded outfits. Use magazines to gather ideas on what's hot and what's not, then update your look according to your own personal style.

Hit your local haberdashery shop and explore a hotbed of possibility. Get inspired to glam up with feathers, ribbons, lace, quirky buttons, or buy rhinestones and studs by the bag, pick out pearl beads, tassel fringe or just about anything else that catches your magpie eye. Then play around with your findings as you try out some of my DIY decorative ideas. You will need to add two extra pieces of equipment to your sewing essentials:

PLIERS
A pair of flat-nosed and round-nosed jewellery-making pliers are indispensable for closing fiddly fastenings like jump rings (cheap packets of these metal connector rings are super nifty for attaching chains, trinkets, links and all sorts of other embellishments). Buy them from a haberdashery or bead shop.

(ANNIE, GET YOUR) GLUE GUN
If you love to customize, you might want to invest in a hot-melt glue gun, which makes light work of sticking down embellishments, fabric and almost everything else. You can even buy glitter and neon glue sticks to load in your gun, perfect for paper crafts (see p. 231 for ideas). Buy one from a craft shop, stationery store or Argos.

NOW LET'S GET CUSTOMIZING...

STUDDING

As a kid, I used to gem up and stud out all my clothes using a BeDazzler, the holy grail of DIY razzle dazzle. Sadly, this dazzling contraption is hard to come by these days, but an extensive range of studs and gems can still be bought from most well-stocked haberdasheries. Get your rocks off and use a handful to jazz up some boring ballet pumps. Or create some epaulettes with felt patches decorated with a selection of studs and rhinestones: use jewellery pliers to fix your gems into place, then sew the patches with a slipstitch on to an old T-shirt.

TASSELS

My favourite novelty trimming, lengths of tassel fringe can create a swinging stir with a Western twist. A short length attached to a chain (connected with jump rings at either end) makes a sensational necklace. Customize a plain T-shirt by sewing some fringe in a V shape from shoulder to shoulder. Or try stitching it down the side seams of shirts, skirts or denim cut-offs. Curtain tassels also make the most excellent earrings and dangly pendants, and try swathing them around your waist as a belt. Make your own tassels using the technique on p. 46 and any yarn, thread, cotton or cording that takes your fancy.

LACE

Lace pieces and trimmings are cheap to buy and can be sewn on to just about anything. Give T-shirts a luxe touch by stitching lace on to the shoulders, or attach as a collar to a plain shift dress. Statement necklaces made from lace look ethereal and can be put together super quick: cut two identical pieces of felt to fit the size and shape of the lace piece, then sew the lace on to one of the felt cut-outs with matching thread and a slipstitch (see p. 62). Cut a length of ribbon long enough to tie in a bow around your neck, cut it in half, then attach to each side of your felt and lace piece with a couple of firm fix stitches to the back. Place the other felt piece over the back, to sandwich the ribbon inside, and use a whipstitch (see p. 61) to secure the two pieces together.

RIBBONS AND BOWS

Bows are timeless and can be knocked up in a matter of minutes, either by hand or on the machine (or try knitting one – see p. 47). Choose a pretty ribbon or a long length of material, fold into a tube and secure with a few stitches. Then pinch the middle and secure with a smaller piece of the same material and a few fix stitches. Try making an over-sized bow for some chic ready-to-wear headgear using a plush velvet, satin, silk or brocade. Make up in the same way using a large piece of fabric, then fix the back on to an old hairband or a metal clasp using your glue gun. Small Dior-style bows look kittenish when used to freshen up the front of an old pair of kicks and can be made up from scrap lengths of ribbon. Or join the mod squad and use thin black ribbons to make snappy bow ties and attach on to a shirt collar for a pretty-but-preppy look.

SEQUINS

Sew sequins together in strips or rows to make gleaming borders for collars, cuffs and pockets – bold yet simple glamour. To sew sequins in strips, bring the needle through the fabric and then through the first sequin, make a backstitch (see p. 61), then go forward and catch another sequin on the needle with the next stitch. Continue, adding more sequins as you go along. To stitch them singly or in small groups, bring the needle up through the fabric, thread a sequin and overcast (see p. 62) it once or twice before securing with a fix stitch at the back.

BEADS

Beads come in all sorts of shapes and sizes and – with a little patience – can be used to embroider detailed arrangements. Experiment with repeated patterns or use shiny iridescent pearl beads for some understated elegance. Sew them on in much the same way as sequins, but use a pen to spot-mark their placement and a fine needle and some invisible thread. Add some sparkling luxury to tired tights with carefully positioned beads. Or why not glam up your woollies by sewing pretty pearls on to your scarves (see pp. 32–3 for how to make your own) and gloves.

✳✳✳✳✳✳ **GET FELTED** ✳✳✳✳✳✳

If you have a particularly itchy or ill-fitting sweater made from 100% wool, why not try your hand at felting? Just wash the sweater on a very hot setting, then tumble dry. This will shrink and matt up your old sweater into a felted fabric ready to be reused in all sorts of ways. Cut up and use to make homespun accessories, like felt flowers attached to hair clasps, rings or combs.

✳✳✳✳✳✳✳✳✳✳✳✳✳✳✳✳✳✳✳✳✳

Junk Box Jewellery

My jewellery box is crammed full of forgotten gems but fortunately, old bits of chain, beads, plastic pearls and trinkets are just begging to be reworked into one-of-a-kind swoonworthy accessories. There's nothing difficult or fiddly about DIY jewellery making, and a pair of pliers and a packet of jump rings (see p. 207) are all you need to get going.

SAFETY PINS

The humble safety pin, iconic emblem of punk rock, is a versatile tool for classic DIY style. Chain them together to make necklaces; string them with beads to make bangles and cuffs. Be a punk princess: buy them in bulk to embellish your clothing too – just pin them in rows against cuffs, collars and shoulders.

CHAINS

Collect old chains or buy new by the metre at a haberdashery (you could even try sourcing chunky but cheap links from more unusual spots like builders' or plumbers' merchants). Make necklaces from chain entwined with lengths of ribbon and adorn with junky jewellery bits and bobs. Chunky chain looks especially good threaded with ribbons and chiffon fabrics to create a statement necklace.

CHARMS

Use trinkets, charms, buttons, bells and beads from old accessories in new customized creations. Make a charm bracelet with some trinkets, jump rings, a small chain and some polyester chiffon. Cut a length of chain to fit snugly but comfortably around your wrist. Then cut a long thin strip of chiffon three times the length of your chain and weave it through the links, leaving two equal lengths on either side to tie around your wrist in a pretty bow. Use the jump rings to attach charms along the chain at intervals.

RINGS

Be a ringleader and create your own bobby-dazzling finger fancies. Invest in some ring blanks (adjustable ring bases with metal tops, available from craft shops) and make dramatic cocktail rings by gluing on charms, beads, the front of an old brooch or a shard of quartz.

ROUND-NOSED PLIERS

FLAT-NOSED PLIERS

BE A RINGLEADER

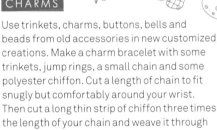

Dye-Craft

Revamp and renovate out-of-date home furnishings or fashions with some simple home-dyeing techniques. I'm a big fan of tie-dyeing, not least because some of my favourite bands were too (stand up Janis and The Grateful Dead), but also because it's so fun to do.

Tie-dyeing is the ancient art of resistant dyeing — the distinctive patterns are created by tying the fabric into folds, pleats, knots and scrunches, which prevents dye from penetrating certain areas. Resistance-dyeing techniques have been around for centuries, all over the world — for example, the intricate Shibori patterns from Japan, or the colourful bold prints and batiks of West Africa. Tie-dye became fashionable in the west in the 60s and 70s, emblematic of the free-spirited Flower Power peace movement.

The best thing about tie-dye is that every piece is a total one-off. When you first start experimenting with tie-dye, the element of surprise will be all part of the fun, but as you get more practised, you will enjoy controlling the designs more closely. Home dyeing is easy, and not nearly as messy as you'd think, so round up your wardrobe, choose a colour and a design and get going on your very own DIY dye job.

TO DYE OR NOT TO DYE?

Natural fibres like cottons, linens and silks dye the best. Whatever fabric you choose must be at least 50% natural fibre for the dye to react successfully. 100% synthetic fabrics will not take dye at all. But be adventurous in what you choose to use: obviously, pale-coloured fabrics show the dye better, but you can even use clothing with pre-printed motifs. I like to liven up old band T-shirts and give them a unique no-one's-got-one-quite-like-mine spin. Have a go with faded denims, leggings, tights, dresses, shorts, bed linen, towels, curtains — you could even try tie-dyeing your smalls for truly psychedelicates.

***** REMEMBER *****

Anything you choose to dye must have been washed at least once before you begin, especially if it is new.

****

EQUIPMENT

DYES

Dylon is my brand of choice — not only is it easy to get hold of (try craft shops, hardware shops, department stores and even some dry cleaners), it's also easy to use. Dylon don't disappoint in the colour stakes, and they have an extensive range — try Burlesque Red next to some Antique Gray, or Velvet Black for some moody grown-up glamour. I also love China Blue and Powder Pink matched with Flamingo Pink or Intense Violet. Don't try to use more than three different colours at one time though, as you might just end up with a brown splodge — not pretty! Dylon fabric dyes come in powder form and should be mixed with warm water before applying — always follow the manufacturer's guidelines.

SALT

Regular table salt is essential to every dye project — it acts as a fixer. Ideally, fabric should be soaked in a salt solution before and after dyeing.

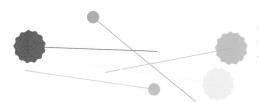

DYE APPLICATION BOTTLES

Any kind of plastic squirt bottle with a secure lid will do. Squeezy sauce bottles are a cheap and cheerful alternative to the specialist bottles you can buy in craft shops. But be warned: some squeezy bottles suffer from leaky-lid syndrome. Be sure your bottle is in good working order before using – there's nothing worse than a DIY dye spillage.

RUBBER BANDS AND STRING

For tying your garments, use rubber bands, string, cotton thread or cord – or better yet, experiment with a combination to master different techniques. Whatever you do, make sure you fasten the ties securely so they do their job properly.

RUBBER GLOVES

To protect your hands. Trust me, you don't want to be scrubbing splodges of dye off your hands for weeks to come. It isn't fun.

BIN BAGS

Use liberally to cover your workspace.

WASHING MACHINE

You will need access to a washing machine to wash your tie-dyed garments with salt and detergent before they are ready to wear.

SINK WITH RUNNING WATER

To rinse out the dyes before you wash the garments in the machine.

* * * * * * * * * * **NB** * * * * * * * * * *

Always wash your new tie-dye creations
with like colours to prevent staining.

* *

HERE'S HOW IT'S DONE:

1. PREPARING

Make sure the item you are dyeing is clean, then soak it in a bucket or a sink with hot water from the tap and 500g of salt for about 15 minutes. Rinse and wring out the cloth until almost dry before laying out ready for tying.

2. TYING

There are a whole bunch of different tie-dye techniques and you can use them singly or combine them, or get really creative and invent your own. Pick a technique from the list on the right, and tie up your fabric ready to be dyed.

3. PREPARING THE DYES

Following the manufacturer's guidelines, prepare all the dyes you have chosen to use (for Dylon dyes, you usually dissolve the powder in hot water in an application bottle and shake vigorously until thoroughly combined).

4. APPLYING THE DYES

Apply one at a time in streaks against the folded pieces of cloth. When the fabric is fully saturated with dye, turn over and do the same on the other side. Leave in a doubled-up plastic bag overnight or for 8–12 hours to let the dyes set.

5. WASHING

The next day, with your rubber gloves on (very important!), remove the items from the plastic bags and – without untying the rubber bands or string – run the cloth under cold running water until the water runs clear. This can take some time, but be patient – it's well worth doing this bit right as it will prevent the colours running and ruining the patterns when you wash them. Now it's time for the big reveal! Wring the cloth out to get rid of excess water, then carefully cut the ties to see your pattern. Put the fabric in the washing machine with 500g of salt (in the drum, not the dispenser) and wash with detergent on a normal 40° cycle. Then leave to dry away from direct heat. (Do not tumble dry.)

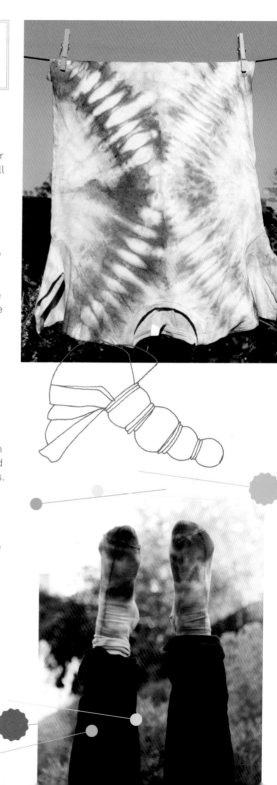

To Dye For
Tie-Dyeing Techniques

MARBLED EFFECT

Scrunch bundles of fabric together, like you would an old newspaper. Secure tightly in a hard ball. This effect looks great on an old pair of jeans or denim cut-offs, and also works well for large items like bed linens – just bunch along the length in sections to create a long firm roll of fabric and secure tightly.

SUNBURST

Gather a section of fabric and slowly rotate to create a pleated swirl. Maintain the shape of the pleats and secure the knotted bundle at different intervals. Looks very effective in the middle of a T-shirt, or try on a bra or bikini – the sunburst circle can be made to any size.

KNOTTING

Pull your fabric into a long point and tie knots in a row all the way down to create stripes. This technique works well for long lengths of fabrics like tights.

TWISTING

Twist the fabric into lengths almost like a skein of wool (it should try to twist back on itself) and secure at regular intervals, including both ends. Looks great on pillowcases and bed sheets.

PLEATING

Fold the fabric accordion style by making regular folds and gathered pleats, then secure at either end and at regular intervals along the fabric strip. Works well with large pieces of fabric.

NECKLACE

Fold a T-shirt in half along the length and use some tailor's chalk to mark a line from the shoulder down to the navel. This will be your guideline. Starting from the navel, make fan folds with your fingers all the way up to the shoulder. Secure all the way along the fabric, keeping your folds in place.

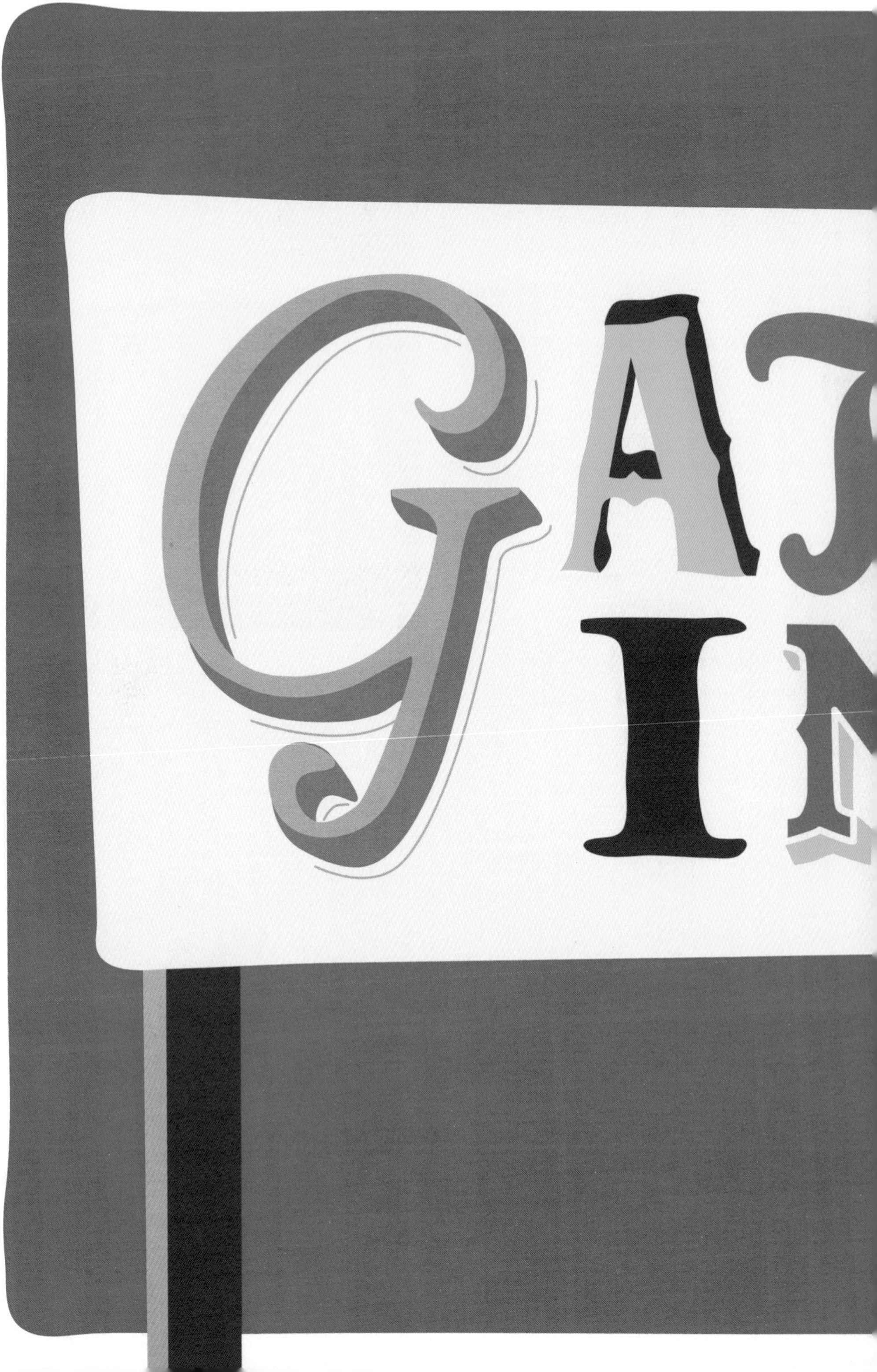

HER
GS »

GATHERINGS

CRAFTING AND COMMUNITY GO
HAND IN HAND – THE LONG AND
SEAMLESS HISTORY OF THE KNITTING
CLUB, THE SEWING CIRCLE AND
THE QUILTING BEE HAS SEEN WOMEN
GATHERING TOGETHER TO SHARE TEA,
STITCHES AND GOSSIP THROUGHOUT
THE AGES. AND THIS LINK BETWEEN
INDIVIDUALS AND THEIR WIDER
CRAFTING COMMUNITY HAS NEVER
BEEN MORE VITAL THAN IT IS TODAY

Domestic skills and crafts were traditionally passed down through the generations; more recently, these skills are being passed between communities instead, as the ever-increasing number of knitting groups and sewing circles cropping up around the world is proving. And really, nothing beats sitting down with a group of friends to share mutual support, skills and crafty know-how.

But as much as these gatherings are good for crafters, the crafts are also good for the gatherings – they provide a focus for people to get together and the social networks that build up around them help to revive a sense of belonging and community spirit. In this way, crafts have a universal power to pull together communities, appealing to male and female, young and old. There are no barriers when it comes to the world of crafts, just a genuine sharing of common interests.

These gatherings can take different forms: quilting groups, knitting circles or even pot-luck parties (see pp. 221–3 for more ideas). Crafters are meeting in all sorts of venues too, getting together to stitch, sew or knit in public, meeting in galleries, cafés, pubs, parks and even on public transport. London knitting group Cast Off famously rode the Circle Line together while holding their weekly knitting meeting. The internet has also become a central hub for crafting communities to congregate – websites, blogs and social networking sites help crafters share tips, techniques, patterns, inspiration and ideas all over the world. Never before have crafters been able to access each other's talents so readily. The internet has helped to jump-start this new creative movement, revolutionizing the way crafters interact with each other by providing a live global platform for crafty communication.

HOW TO ORGANIZE A CRAFTING CLUB

Share your passion with like-minded friends by organizing and hosting your own crafting meets – it's hugely rewarding, not to mention lots of fun.

If your immediate circle of friends are craft phobic (sadly, my sister wouldn't be seen dead anywhere near a needle and thread), it will give you the opportunity to make a whole new network of friends who do share your love of craft. Or if you're already part of a community club that meets up regularly, why not suggest setting up a sub-group? Setting up a crafting group is easy; all you need is a little time, dedication and organization. Here's how you do it.

GET THE WORD ON THE STREET

Get online and spread the word via your blog, website, twitter or facebook page that you are looking for people to join a new craft club. Extend the invitation to your immediate community by making some fliers (hand-written or cut-and-paste photocopied) or even an intriguing promotional 'zine (see p. 232) and hitting the streets to distribute them in coffee shops, clothing stores, hang-outs and on community notice boards. When I started the Shoreditch Sisters, I was amazed by the overwhelming response from girls I had never met, eager to join in and be part of the fun. Which gave me the chance to meet all sorts of interesting new people I may never have crossed paths with were it not for our mutual love of sewing and crafts.

CHOOSE A NAME

Have a brainstorm to come up with a fun name for your club; how about 'Knit-Wits' or 'Knitter-Natters' for a knitting club, and maybe 'Material Girls' or 'Stitching Sisters' for a sewing group? Or try to think of something that makes reference to your local area. Make sure it's snappy and start using it immediately.

FIND A VENUE

This can often be tricky – you want a space that is not only cheap or even free but also spacious enough for the entire group to get crafting. A village hall or a public meeting house can usually be secured for next to nothing. Or, if the club is small enough, host meetings at a member's house. For bigger groups, a bar or pub with a function room may be willing to let you use the space for free during off-peak hours. Make sure you avoid anywhere too lively, or you will be distracted from the work at hand. Working facilities are another consideration – how many tables and chairs are available, is the lighting good enough and how about power sockets for plugging in sewing machines?

SET A DATE

Run your club at the same time and on the same day every week or month to avoid confusion over dates and times. People are busy, so don't expect everyone to turn up to every session; it's best to think of them as drop-ins, which sets a more relaxed tone. Keep members up to date with round-robin emails or set up a blog, facebook or myspace page to act as a notice board.

SEWING TOOLS

If you plan on doing any large-scale work, you will more than likely need to use a sewing machine at some point – perhaps one of your members may be willing to lend the use of their own machine. Ask each member to bring their own sewing kits with all the essentials: needles, scissors, pins, tape measure and a notebook and pen for jotting down ideas.

MATERIALS

There will be costs involved if you need large amounts of fabric and materials to complete a project, but worry not – there are ways of cutting these down considerably. In my experience, most people are happy to bring along some of their excess stash to share among the group. It may also be worth getting in touch with any local textile, fashion or furnishings businesses that may donate end-of-roll and end-of-season fabrics or materials for a worthy cause. Pound the pavement (rather than the phone book) and be brave – making face-to-face contact will work wonders when building and sustaining these kinds of connections.

SHARE SKILLS

One of the best things about craft clubs is the potential for skill sharing. Play on each other's strengths: if someone is skilled at freehand drawing, get them designing appliqué patterns, or if you have a champion needlewoman in your midst, put her in charge of finishing touches.

PROJECTS

So what are you going to make? This is the exciting part, so get your heads together and have a brainstorm. Try stitching a banner for a local craft fair, shop or event. Make pretty pincushions (see p. 70) to sell at a fête or even put your kitchen skills to the test and start a cake-and-chutney stall (see pp. 113–19, 139–47 for recipes). Or why not put your needles to good use and craft for charity? Non-profit organizations are always more than grateful for donations like scarves for homeless shelters, toys for vulnerable children, blankets for animal shelters or knitted hats for sailors and fishermen (see 'Address Book', p. 236).

BLOCK PARTY — HOST YOUR OWN QUILTING BEE

Patchwork has long been associated with friendship and sharing, whether materials, skills, support or the quilts themselves.

Quilting parties, or 'bees' as they are known in America, are still popular social occasions and are a great excuse for gathering friends together for a good old-fashioned gossip. They are also practical – a quilt will grow more rapidly the more people are working on it. Setting up your own quilting group is no different from organizing a craft club (as above). However, as you will probably be working on a large-scale group project, you should have someone in charge, to motivate, delegate tasks and instruct the group. So the first thing you need to do is to appoint at least one or two people to be in charge of the following:

- Finding a venue
- Organizing meet-ups and supervising the sessions
- Planning and designing the quilt
- Buying the fabric and organizing the stash
- Preparing and cutting out required templates and fabrics
- Joining the blocks together
- Lining and backing the work

If you don't have a particular project in mind, consider making a patchwork quilt to sell at a charity event to raise money for a cause that's important to the group. Or why not create a quilt that commemorates the inauguration of your group that you can hang proudly at every meet? Try making a block quilt, made up of individual pieced squares joined together to form one large unit. Perfect for collaborative quilting (and the ultimate friendship quilts), the individual squares of a block quilt can simply be sewn together edge-to-edge and then framed within a bound border.

HOW TO WORK A BLOCK QUILT

As a block quilt is built up entirely of squares, you'll need some graph paper to design your own and work out how many squares to make. You also have to decide what size you want your individual squares to be. Most standard block templates tend to be 20–25 cm but tailor to suit your individual requirements.

Pick your fabric – for quilts that are to be hung up and displayed, a heavy, durable foundation fabric like calico or cotton mattress ticking would work best – then get cutting! Using a template – which you can either buy or make yourself from some stiff card or lightweight plastic – cut the required number of square blocks from your chosen foundation fabric before sharing them out for members to decorate as they like.

Use your first meet-up to plan the design of your quilt and cut up the squares, then allow everyone to finish decorating their individual blocks at home. Set a deadline for when the blocks must be finished and ask everyone to sign the individual block patch they made. Spend the next session focusing on joining the blocks to assemble into the final quilt composition, then sew the patches together (see 'Patchwork', p. 80).

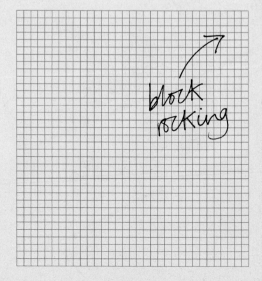

block ticking

NEEDLE EXCHANGE – HOST YOUR OWN CRAFT SWAP-SHOP

Make no bones about it, we all know that hoarding comes with the territory for many crafters, so why not set up a craft market with friends to share some thrifty fun? Crafting swaps work best as one-off events, as people are more inclined to make an effort to get involved and organize their excess stockpiles and supplies ready for a major haul-out. Here are some fun ideas for getting the most out of your crafting community.

RECIPE EXCHANGE

Host a pot-luck tea, cake and recipe exchange. Get your guests to bring their prize-winning cake or cookie recipes to swap, and sample each other's baked goodies as well. The Shoreditch Sisters held a cake extravaganza with a friendly bake-off (see p. 126 for the full story) and wrote down all our recipes to be compiled into a one-off 'zine (see p. 232). Why not do the same using recipes gathered from your friends and family?

FABRIC EXCHANGE

Either by post or by party, fabric exchanges are a great way to get hold of new materials. Host a party (tea parties are always popular, see p. 222) and invite friends and family to bring along any craft goodies they no longer need, then see what bartering can be done to bag yourself a bargain. In my experience, older relatives are more than happy to dispense with crafting clobber that has been languishing in a dusty attic. I have been given countless bits and bobs over the years and I'm always keen to swap stacks of knitting patterns for excess metres of fabric or bountiful bags of buttons.

FREE

SWAP SHOP

BARGAIN

PARTY CRAFTS— LET THE GOOD TIMES ROLL

Gatherings and celebrations are the threads that hold the fabric of communities together and are also the perfect opportunity for you to get crafty with your party antics.

So do things a little differently for your next get-together and have a knitting picnic or an after-hours tea dance with homemade cakes (see p. 112). If you're going to party, you might as well be crafty while you're at it.

TEA PARTIES

My very first birthday saw a tea party to rival all tea parties and my initiation into what was to become a lifelong passion. My mum, who takes the planning of tea parties very seriously, used to throw me and my sister utterly extravagant parties, always in a riot of colour. Tables heaved with an assortment of sandwiches, cakes, biscuits, sweeties, streamers, party poppers, Smarties sprinkled like confetti; there were balloons everywhere you looked and the music was amped up to eleven. At my first birthday bash, dolled up to the nines in my very first polka-dot frock (to match the red and white polka-dot tablecloth, napkins, paper cups and plates), I was something of a bewildered bystander to my parents' raucous revelry as my first tea party turned into an all night rave-up.

So turn traditional afternoon tea on its head the next time you celebrate and host your own after-dark tea party. Invite guests to attend no earlier then 8pm, and sip pink fizzy wine from delicate floral china teacups, served with a selection of classic tea-party fare. Think Battenberg cake, Jammie Dodgers and Tunnock's Tea Cakes, accompanied by a spread of decorative and delicately cut sandwiches. Then bop till you drop.

LIFE'S A PICNIC

Every summer, when the English weather permits, the Shoreditch Sisters host an annual 'Pot Luck in the Park' picnic. It's one of the few times during the year we invite the menfolk to join in our WI fun, and members are encouraged to invite boyfriends, brothers, dads and even grandads to come down and meet the gang. We string up the bunting, have the ghetto blaster blaring and sample each other's finest picnic fare. And if we're lucky, we may have one or two travelling minstrel friends come and serenade us. Organize a knitting picnic and enjoy the click-clacking of needles while you nibble on homemade cakes and biscuits. Or get everyone to bring their bikes and arrange an en masse cycle to your picnic spot, crossing your fingers for good weather.

CRAFTERNOON

Hold an informal crafternoon party with friends on a lazy Sunday afternoon and get your crew down to hang out and make all sorts of handy handmade bits and bobs. You could have a DIY fashion day, stitching beads, sequins and all sorts of other shiny embellishments to worn-out gear (see p. 207 for customizing ideas).

DRESSED TO A TEA – DECORATIVE SANDWICHES

Dress up your tea table and add variety to your standard sandwich smorgasbord by crafting fancy finger food using decadent fillings for some dainty charm. Experiment with pinwheels, chessboard or fancy-cut sandwich shapes. Decorate with hand-drawn sandwich flags (a tiny paper flag attached to a toothpick with some Sellotape) describing the fillings and sprinkle with home-grown mustard and cress (see pp. 156–7). If you're making up sandwiches in advance, wrap your pre-cut dainties in some cling film and greaseproof paper and put in the fridge, leaving the finishing touches till the guests arrive.

••• Buttering Up •••

Here's a little tip for making perfectly formed sandwiches. Before assembling, make sure the butter is at room temperature and then cream with a fork – this will help it to spread more evenly on the bread. Tea-party sandwiches should always be delicate, so use very thin slices of bread, always cut off the crusts and butter lightly.

••• Teatime Classic •••

The classic cucumber sandwich should never be dismissed as being too simple – it is truly delicious. Make your cucumber fancies on thin white crustless slices of bread spread with a thin layer of butter and a sprinkle of salt and pepper, layered with very finely cut thins of cucumber. Traditionally, these sandwiches are cut into very small triangles or fingers.

FANCY-CUT

Use metal cookie cutters in assorted shapes to create ever-so-fancy sandwiches. For a more economical alternative, use a sharp knife to cut them into mini squares, diamonds or fingers instead. Use brown or white bread, or a mixture of both for a two-tone effect.

PINWHEELS

Cut off the crusts from very thin slices of soft white or brown bread and use a rolling pin to flatten before spreading with softened butter and your chosen filling. Then roll the sandwiches up like Swiss rolls, tightly but without squeezing, which will ruin their shape. Wrap in cling film and store in the fridge until you're ready to roll, then cut into neat slices using a clean sharp knife.

CHESSBOARD

These neat little sandwiches resemble a chessboard when laid out together and are made using contrasting brown and white slices of bread. Cut an equal number of slices of brown and white bread, butter up and add your fillings. Assemble each sandwich using a slice of brown on top of a slice of white, then cut into four squares. Lay the squares out in a chessboard pattern on the plate.

TRIPLE-DECKER

For the ultimate in sandwich decadence, butter a slice of white bread, spread on a filling, then cover with a buttered slice of brown bread. Butter the top of the brown slice, spread on another filling then top with another slice of buttered white. Finally, slice into whatever shape takes your fancy.

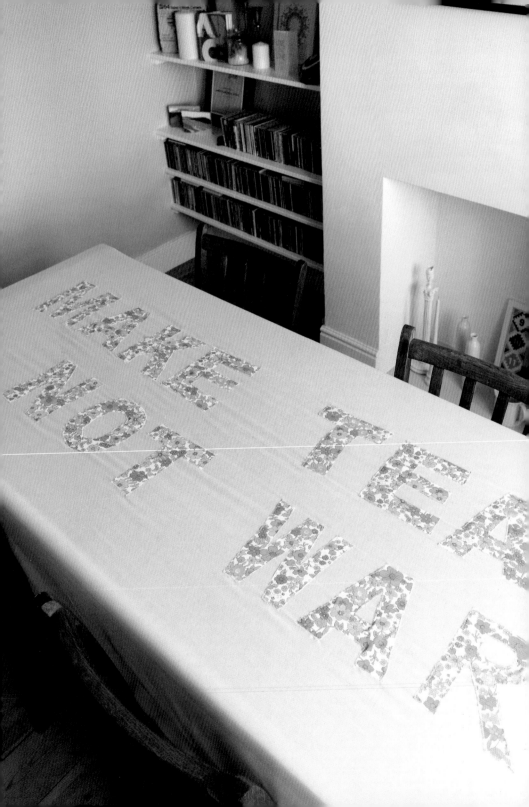

MAKE TEA NOT WAR TABLECLOTH

No tea party of mine is ever complete without a pretty tablecloth, and what better way to set the tone for your own tea table than with this 'Make Tea Not War' appliqué design?

The hard-and-fast rule for making this pretty tablecloth (or any other you might fancy) is to always use the widest length of fabric you can find to keep seams and hems to a minimum. Often a plain ready-made tablecloth or flat bed sheet will be your best bet.

BEFORE YOU BEGIN:

MEASUREMENTS – determine what size your tablecloth should be. Measure your table, then work out how much of a drop you want (how much cloth drapes over the side of your table); usually 20–30 cm should do it. As the drop will hang on all four sides of the table, multiply this measurement by two and add to both your width and length measurements. And remember, if you're making your tablecloth from scratch, you will also have to factor in hem allowances. Standard tablecloth hems are turned under twice and measure about 4 cm in total, so don't forget to add this on to your final measurement.

TEMPLATES – whatever phrase you choose to adorn your tablecloth with ('Make Tea Not War' or something that's meaningful to you), you'll need to make some paper templates for cutting out the letters. If you're a skilled freehand drawer, simply draw the letters on to some paper and cut out. Otherwise, type out your phrase on the computer and enlarge the letters to at least 10 cm tall before printing and cutting out to make your templates.

YOU WILL NEED:

- Plain fabric (a flat sheet, tablecloth or piece of fabric)
- Paper templates for 10 cm lettering
- Scrap fabrics in contrasting colours for the appliqué lettering
- Pins
- Scissors – to cut fabric and paper
- Sewing machine
- Iron

MAKING:

1. First wash your tablecloth fabric to prevent any shrinkage from interfering with your design. Then press and fold the fabric into four and press again to establish the centrefold. This will make it easier to position your appliqué letters.

2. If you are using a large length of fabric (not a tablecloth or sheet), you need to neaten the raw edges with a double hem. To do this, turn the fabric under on all sides 1 cm and press, turn another 3 cm, press again and either pin or tack the seam into place. Topstitch the hems down on the machine (see p. 76), sewing as close to the seam edge as possible, and mitre the corners neatly (see p. 68).

3. Use your templates to mark and cut out fabric letters in contrasting colours and patterns. Arrange the letters in the middle of the tablecloth's longest edge, starting at least 8 cm from the corner and leaving 8 cm gaps between each word. Pin or tack each letter into place. Stitch the letters down on the sewing machine using zigzag, satin or straight stitching (see p. 76).

4. Give the tablecloth one final press, then invite your friends round for some tea!

BUNTING

When life throws you scraps, make bunting! Nothing says 'party time' like a garland of colourful flags, and bunting brings instant charm to any gathering. Cut fabric, felt or paper to make flags in unusual shapes or craft them from old crochet or knitted squares. I like to personalize bunting with cut-out appliqué lettering and motifs and give it away to friends and family. And as bunting can be used over and over again, it will be something to treasure for years to come.

To make your own bunting, you'll first need a template. Use a ruler and a pencil and the measurements below to draw a triangle with two equal sides on to a piece of paper or card stock. Then cut out and voila! – you have your very own bunting flag template.

LAZY GAL BUNTING

Got only minutes to spare? Whip up this lazy gal bunting using just single-sided flags for some super swift, cheap and cheerful party décor.

YOU WILL NEED:

- Paper template
- Scrap cotton fabrics
- Pinking shears
- 5 cm binding tape
- Pins
- Sewing machine
- Iron

MAKING:

1. Use your template to cut out enough fabric flags to fit along your binding tape. Make sure the fabrics have been ironed before cutting and use pinking shears to ensure a ravel-free edge.

2. If it isn't already creased down the centre, fold your binding tape in half lengthwise and press. Then position your flags within the fold of the binding and pin at regular intervals along the length of the tape. Leave 10 cm free at either end to make loops for hanging.

3. Using matching thread and a straight stitch on the machine (see p. 76), sew along the entire length of the tape as close to the edge as you can, catching each flag as you go.

4. Finally, stitch the hanging loops into place, by folding the tape back to the point where the last flag was attached and making a few fix stitches (see p. 62) to keep it in place. A final press to neaten and you're done!

FLAG SIZES

SMALL	MEDIUM	LARGE
16 cm wide x 20 cm high	20 cm wide x 25 cm high	25 cm wide x 30 cm high

fancy fabric
bunting

FANCY FABRIC BUNTING

This is a slightly more time-consuming way to make bunting, but you get a more professional finish (good for gifts). And to give your bunting a really personal touch, appliqué some lettering on to the flags, or perhaps add a little pompom trim for some frivolous fancy edging.

YOU WILL NEED:

- Paper template
- Scrap cotton fabrics
- Fabric scissors
- Pins
- 5 cm binding tape
- Sewing machine
- Embellishments – felt for appliqué lettering or decorative trims of your choice
- Iron

MAKING:

1. Cut out fabric flags using your template, adding an extra 6 mm to each side for a seam allowance. Each flag is made from two pieces of fabric sewn together, so as you cut, pin the flags into pairs with right sides facing together. Continue until you have enough flags to fit along the tape.

2. If you want to add some embellishment to the flag fronts, do so now, before you sew up the side seams. If you're using felt, cut out your preferred motifs (initials work well), then pin to the front and either sew down by hand using a blanket stitch (see p. 62) or on the machine with a zigzag, satin or straight stitch (see p. 76).

3. With the flags paired up and pinned with right sides facing together, sew the two long sides together (with a 6mm seam allowance) using a straight stitch on the machine. Leave the top open. Snip the tip of each flag, then turn right side out, work the tip out to a point and press.

4. If it isn't already folded, make a crease down the centre of your bias tape by folding it in half lengthwise and pressing. Working about 12.5 cm in from the end of the tape, position each flag within the fold of the binding and pin at regular intervals. If you fancy adding some decorative trim to the tape, do so now. Then on the machine using a straight stitch, sew along the entire length of the tape as close to the edge as you can, catching each flag as you go. Finally, stitch the hanging loops into place, by folding the tape back to the point where the last flag was attached and making a few fixing odd stitches (see p. 62) to keep it in place.

I ♥ FELT BUNTING

Surprise your valentine or show a friend some heartfelt thanks with a string of this adorable bunting. Not a romantic? Not to worry, swap the hearts for circles, stars, Christmas trees – you name it, anything goes! I like the hearts because they are not only super sweet but also super simple to cut out – you don't even need a template. Just fold a square of felt in half, then cut half a heart against the folded edge, unfold and you have a perfectly formed heart. Felt bunting is not as hard wearing as the fabric variety so it's best kept indoors.

YOU WILL NEED:

- Pink and red felt (or any combinations of colours you fancy)
- Invisible thread
- Fabric scissors
- Pins
- Sewing machine

MAKING:

1. Figure out how long you want your bunting to be, then cut out enough different-sized and -coloured felt hearts to fit.

2. Use good-quality invisible thread to chain sew the hearts together to create one continuous length of bunting. To begin, place the first heart widthwise towards the presser foot and needle and sew using a straight stitch (see p. 76) through the middle of the heart. When you get to the end, place another heart directly against the edge of the last and continue sewing in the same way. Continue sewing the hearts edge to edge until you get to your last.

3. To hang the bunting, either drape as a garland without hangers, or you could add a couple of loops to the backs of the first and the last hearts in the string. Cut out two 8cm lengths of binding tape, fold in half, then sew to the edge of the hearts with some sturdy fix stitches (see p. 62).

THAT'S A WRAP

When your homemade creations are intended as gifts, don't spoil the show with your wrapping. The outside should inspire as much wonder as the loveliness waiting within. Here are some ideas to make your presents almost too good to unwrap:

DOILIES – Stick a paper doily (shop-bought or even make your own; I know I don't need to show you how) on top of your parcel before tying up with ribbon or string.

PAPER BOWS – Use any kind of scrap paper to make a concertina bow which you can then either tape on to your parcel or hole punch through the centre to tie on with some yarn or ribbon.

YARN – Wrap your parcel in yarn instead of boring old string (or expensive ribbon) and style up with a pair of pompoms (see p. 48) instead of a bow.

TRIMMINGS – Leftover scraps of ribbons and other pretty trims make perfect embellishments glued to the front of your packages.

BROWN PAPER – Always keep a roll of brown wrapping paper to hand; it's super cheap and is perfect for last-minute gift-wrapping. It also looks great covered in text handwritten with sharpies or thick felt tips.

TISSUE FLOWERS – So simple yet so darling. Make a rose from a long strip of tissue paper. Fold the tissue in half lengthwise but don't crease the fold, then roll up the strip starting at one end and holding the bottom edge while twisting to create a flower shape. Stick to your parcel with a dab of glue or make a few to group together.

SEWING PATTERNS – Old sewing patterns make a lovely alternative to tissue paper and can be picked up cheaply at charity shops and car boot sales.

LUGGAGE LABELS – Make your own from coloured card or any other kind of paper (magazine cuttings work well for fashion-conscious friends). Trim to shape and hole punch (reinforce with a white eyelet sticker if you have one), then decorate with alphabet ink stamps, Letraset letters or felt tips. Don't underestimate the power of penmanship – a quirky handwritten sentiment can sometimes make all the difference.

••• ALL STITCHED UP •••

Now you're wrapped and ready to go, make a hand-stitched card for an extra crafted touch. Fold some thick paper into a basic card, then, with a pencil, draw a simple design on the front – a heart, a star or an initial would be perfect. With a pin, prick through from the front to the back of the card all the way along your pencil line at regular intervals at least 6 mm apart. Erase your pencil marks. Thread a hand-sewing needle with some contrasting thread and weave in and out of the pin pricks before securing at the back of the card with a knot.

MINI 'ZINE MANIA

Get on the scene and make your own mini 'zine to promote a crafting group, meeting, party or any other gathering. Fanzines were notoriously adopted by the DIY punk and Riot Grrrl movements, scribbled on just about every subject under the sun. Giving voice to a previously unheard underground, 'zines became a creatively explosive way to share ideas and opinions.

First think of a subject: will your 'zine be a dear-diary manifesto, a collection of your favourite recipes or a homage to your favourite band? Come up with an eye-catching title. You want to draw people in and excite their interest immediately, so something funny or even shocking will be irresistible. Then ...

2. Fold the paper back in half widthwise and use a pair of scissors to cut from the centre fold to the next fold.

3. Open the paper up again, then fold in half lengthwise. Holding one end of the paper in each hand, bring your hands together to push the paper into a cross shape. The point at which your fingertips meet will be the spine of the booklet. Fold the paper around to create a book shape and crease the spine with a fingernail. You should now have a front cover and a back cover with two pages in between. Now start planning layout and content. The pages are small, so your ideas will have to be concentrated. Draw, design, illustrate or write whatever you want. Use a photocopier to resize text and images that you can then cut out and glue to your 'zine.

4. Once you've designed all sixteen pages, get going photocopying your first print run, or go one step further and get your 'zine printed at a copy shop.

YOU WILL NEED:

- 1 sheet of A4 paper
- Scrap paper
- Pens
- Paper scissors
- Glue
- Photocopier (optional)

MAKING:

1. Fold the A4 paper in half three times, creasing the edges with a fingernail as you go. Unfold and take a look at your paper – it should be creased into eight small rectangles (these will be your pages). Flip the paper over and fold again, to reinforce the creases.

cut here

Read all about it!

GIRLS JUST WANT TO HAVE FUN –
HOW TO RUN A MODERN WI GROUP

You go girls

Starting up your own Women's Institute chapter can be a life-changing decision – you will get the hard work, time and energy you put into it repaid threefold in the fun to be had and the friendships made.

So if you have some extra time on your hands, think about starting up a group in your own town with some friends. Here's all the insider knowledge you'll need to set up and run your very own fully accredited branch. And as someone who has made many mistakes but also had plenty of small victories in my adventures as a WI instigator, I hope I can give it to you straight.

HOW TO START A WI GROUP

Now, there is a world of difference between joining the WI and starting a WI group. Once you commit to the latter, you better be ready for a rollercoaster of a ride. Don't enter into the decision lightly – it will take up a lot of time, effort and organizational power.

Begin by checking out your local area for any established WI chapters. If there aren't any, you have no excuse not to start one. However, if there are one or two already, try to figure out why you don't want to join them. Whatever the reason, be clear on what it is you are looking for that the existing groups are not offering. (I only make a point of this because your local WI advisor will ask you the exact same question.) You will have to rope in some friends to form a committee – you need at least five people willing to pay the membership subscription (£30 a year) upfront to open a new branch of the WI. Finding a venue and setting a time and date for your monthly meetings will be your next task. A weekday evening is best, so as not to clash with weekend diversions – most members will enjoy the novelty of attending the meetings straight from work once a month. Try to book the meetings at least three months in advance; use your contacts and try to get people to do things for free – the WI is a charity, after all.

Then organize your first official public meeting. Pick an activity or a speaker that will appeal to a broad spectrum of people and strikes the balance between informative and recreational. Now spread the word. Make a promotional flier, pamphlet or fanzine (see opposite), something both fun and informative to get people excited about coming. Include all the relevant info (date, time and venue), a bit of blurb about your group, contact details and web address.

Remember, you will have people who have paid money to be part of this organization relying on you to fulfil their investment. So I cannot stress how important it is to have a reliable committee group to support you. You will need their help as you pool all your energies and resources together to keep the group running as effortlessly as possible. Don't forget to have monthly committee meetings so you can all catch up and plan the year's events.

ADDRESS BOOK

Here's a list of my favourite crafty haunts. Because I'm a London girl, most are in the capital, but don't worry if you don't live in the big smoke – many of them sell their wares or promote their services online. And don't forget to check out your own local area for craft shops or classes – the handmade revolution is growing fast.

HABERDASHERY HOT SPOTS

Kleins
5 Noel Street
London
W1F 8GD
020 7437 6162
www.kleins.co.uk

Best selection of fringing and tassels by the metre I've seen anywhere. And lots of other haberdashery trimmings: pipe cleaners, beads (including fuzzy pompom beads), buttons, feathers, appliqué patches, zips – the list goes on.

MacCulloch & Wallis
25–6 Dering Street
London
W1A 1AT
020 7629 0311
www.macculloch-wallis.co.uk

Proper old-fashioned fabric and haberdashery shop – they stock everything! With one whole floor devoted to ribbons and bias binding. You can't get much better than that.

John Lewis
Oxford Street
London
W1A 1EX
020 7629 7711
www.johnlewis.com

Still one of the best places to go for all your sewing and knitting needs. I am in love with their mini sewing machines (£50 at time of writing). John Lewis have stores around the country, but not all of them have a haberdashery department, so check before you make a special visit.

V V Rouleaux
102 Marylebone Lane
London
W1U 2QD
020 7224 5179
www.vvrouleaux.com

The best place to source ribbons and trims. Can be a bit pricey, but totally worth it if you've got a bit of spare cash to treat yourself or you are looking for some inspiration.

The Button Queen
19 Marylebone Lane
London
W1V 2NF
020 7935 1505
www.thebuttonqueen.co.uk

Pick up your button booty at this delightful one-stop button shop, where you will find rare and unusual vintage and modern buttons galore.

Creative Beadcraft
20 Beak Street
London
W1F 9RE
020 7629 9964
www.creativebeadcraft.co.uk

For chains, beads, acrylic rhinestones, Swarovski crystals and all sorts of other jewellery-making goodies. This shop is usually awash with London's fashion students stocking up on supplies, so be prepared for a crowd.

DYE

www.dylon.co.uk

See Dylon's website for a list of stockists. Most craft, haberdashery and art shops stock a good selection of Dylon colours, as do homeware and hardware stores.

KNITTING SHOPS

All the Fun of the Fair
3rd Floor
8 Kingly Court
Carnaby Street
London
W1B 5PW
020 7287 2303
www.allthefunofthefair.bigcartel.com

Small but seriously cute yarn and haberdashery shop in London's historic Carnaby Street. They sell hand-knitted cakes, doughnuts and hilarious tea cosies, as well as a great selection of novelty crafting items like pompom and yo-yo makers, loads of fun buttons and sewing-themed charms.

Prick Your Finger
260 Globe Road
London
E2 0JD
020 8981 2560
www.prickyourfinger.com

Quirky East End knitting boutique with famously fabulous window displays. Founders of London knitting group Cast Off, who hold workshops and classes for all knitters and crotchet makers.

I Knit
106 Lower Marsh
London
SE1 7AB
020 7261 1338
www.iknit.org.uk

Just round the corner from Waterloo station, this knitting shop also runs twice-weekly knitting meets and even an annual knitting weekender!

Loop
15 Camden Passage
London
N1 8EA
020 7288 1160
www.loopknitting.com

Lovely knitting boutique in Islington, stocking knitting and crotchet patterns and high quality yarns.

FABRIC SHOPS

Beyond Fabrics
67 Columbia Road
London
E2 7RG
020 7729 5449
www.beyond-fabrics.com

One of my favourite fabric shops in London – they stock a lovely range of patterned cottons, including reproduction retro prints like ditzy 1930s florals, sold in fat quarters and jelly rolls. Perfect for patchwork!

Dalston Mill Fabrics
69–73 Ridley Road
London
E8 2NP
020 7249 4129
www.dalstonmillfabrics.co.uk

A real Aladdin's cave, this shop has a fantastic selection of fabrics as well as a brilliant little haberdashery section at the back selling Dylon dye, ribbons, trimmings, threads and a super selection of buttons.

Goldhawk Road
Shepherds Bush
London
W12

Best selection of fabric shops all in one London locale. The cluster of shops along the Goldhawk Road in Shepherds Bush is where you'll see all the fashion students picking up bargains and you should always be able to strike a good deal if you haggle.

Fabrics Galore
52–4 Lavender Hill
London
SW11 5RH
020 7738 9589
www.fabricsgalore.co.uk

Great for patchwork fabrics, as they have a lovely selection of printed 100% cottons. But best of all, they specialize in end-of-line fabrics sold at rock-bottom prices – everything from Liberty to leopard print!

SEWING MACHINES

www.janome.co.uk

I swear by my Janome sewing machine (model 2522LE, £349 at time of writing). Buy one from a Janome retailer (some sell online) or try John Lewis. And don't forget to check out their list of nationwide sewing courses.

KITCHENCRAFT

www.robertdyas.co.uk

A fantastic high-street homeware shop. Take a trip down to your local Robert Dyas to fulfil all of your gardening, jam making and baking needs. And they have the best selection of deliciously retro Tala kitchenware.

www.lakeland.co.uk

The home of creative kitchenware – buy all your baking, icing and jam-making equipment here. They have a brilliant selection of glass Kilner jars (perfect for potting your body scrubs too).

www.jamjarshop.com

All the jam-making equipment you'll ever need, including polka-dot jam lids and ready-made stick-on labels. Deluxe kits can be sent straight to the door of any jam-making enthusiast.

DIY BEAUTY SUPPLIES

G Baldwin & Co.
171–3 Walworth Road
London
SE17 1RW
020 7703 5550
www.baldwins.co.uk

Old-fashioned apothecary and London's oldest herbalist. Visit the extensive shop on the Walworth Road, order a catalogue or shop online.

www.nealsyardremedies.com

My go-to place for aromatherapy oils, beeswax and one of the best orange flower waters made anywhere. Neal's Yard Remedies have stores across the country; see their website for one near you.

www.aromatic.co.uk

Great online shop selling everything you'll need to get you started, including some of the best natural fragrance oils. They also provide lots of free advice and tips.

URBAN FARMS
For some green-fingered kicks, check out your local city farm to see if you can help out. Here are my London favourites:

www.hackneycityfarm.co.uk
www.spitalfieldscityfarm.org
www.vauxhallcityfarm.org

MARKETS
The best place to source your vintage goodies is a market; you can bag yourself bargains galore. Here are my favourite market hang-outs:

Brick Lane Market
Shoreditch
London
E1
www.visitbricklane.org

Sunday
Lots of different sub-sections and mini markets make up this bustling London market. Check out the Sunday Up Market (www.sundayupmarket.co.uk) held in an indoor car park at 91 Brick Lane, where local designers sell their handmade and vintage wares.

Cabbages and Frocks Market
St Marylebone Parish Church Grounds
Marylebone High Street
NW1 5LT
www.cabbagesandfrocks.co.uk

Saturday, 11am–5pm
Browse retro and vintage homewares and clothing while sampling locally made cupcakes and baked treats.

Camden Passage Market
Camden Passage
London
N1 5ED
www.camdenpassageislington.co.uk

Saturday
Visit this small but perfectly formed little market behind Upper Street in Islington for vintage, fashion, craft and antiques.

Columbia Road Flower Market
Columbia Road
London
E2 7RG
www.columbiaroad.info

Sunday
Take a stroll down Columbia Road in Shoreditch on a Sunday for loads of floral bargains, especially if you hit the sellers as they are packing up for the day (2pm-ish.) And check out Vintage Heaven at 82 Columbia Road for beautiful vintage crockery and linens or rest up at their Cakehole Café.

Greenwich Market
Greenwich
London
SE10 9HZ
www.greenwichmarket.net

Saturday and Sunday
For local arts and crafts, and check out nearby Deptford Markets (Deptford High Street, Douglas Way and Griffin Square) on a Saturday for junky bric-a-brac and a flea market feel – plenty of hidden gems to be found.

Portobello Market
Portobello Road
London
W10
www.portobellomarket.org

Friday, Saturday, Sunday
Check out the world-famous Portobello Market on Friday for all your vintage goodies (without the crowds who descend on Saturdays).

Spitalfields Antiques Market
Spital Square
London
E1
www.visitspitalfields.com/stalls/
antiques

Thursday
Recently redeveloped,
Spitalfields Market (every day
but Saturday) has sadly lost a
lot of its chaotic charm, but the
antiques market is still a great
place to source all sorts of vintage
ware. Buy cheap bags of broken
jewellery and vintage buttons,
not to mention loads of second-
hand homeware, crockery,
clothes and old magazines.

CRAFT HUBS

Drink Shop and Do
9 Caledonian Road
Kings Cross
London
N1 9DX
www.drinkshopdo.com

Vintage-style café and shop
selling designer crafts and retro
homewares. You can drink tea
from a vintage tea set and munch
homemade cakes while you
craft or play games.

Homemade London
21 Seymour Place
London
W1H 5BH
www.homemadelondon.com

Lovely little crafting salon
and sewing café in the heart
of London's West End.

Fabrication
7 Broadway Market
London
E8 4PH
020 7275 8043
www.fabrications1.co.uk

A studio, shop and gallery all rolled
into one. The lovely owner, Barley
Massey, always has time for a chat
and answers to crafty questions.
They stock a good selection of
yarns, needles, books and locally
designed craft kits, and they also
run craft classes on a regular basis.

Liberty Sewing School
Liberty
Regent Street
London
W1B 5AH
020 7734 1234
www.liberty.co.uk

Who can resist visiting Liberty's
haberdashery department? Well,
now they have a sewing school too.
Although prices are fairly steep (£50
per person per workshop), there's a
lot to be said for learning to sew at
one of London's most prestigious
institutions.

Make Lounge
49–51 Barnsbury Street
London
N1 1TP
020 7609 0275
www.themakelounge.com

Crafting workshops at a shop in
Islington selling fabric and all sorts
of sewing supplies. Take a class in
your sewing or stitching skills – or
why not try soap making, biscuit
decorating or fascinator making?

The Create Place
29 Old Ford Road
London
E2 9PJ
www.backtobasicsartsandcrafts.
blogspot.com

This great little independent
non-profit workshop run by
volunteers offers all sorts of crafty
classes, clubs, drop-in sessions
and even open studio time.

Sweat Shop
13 Rue Lucien Sampaix
75010 Paris
www.sweatshopparis.com

If you happen to find yourself in
Paris, check out this lovely little
sewing shop – you can rent a sewing
machine for the day
and stitch in style.

THE WOMEN'S INSTITUTE

To find out more about the WI,
contact their head office directly
or check out their website.

**National Federation
of Women's Institutes**
104 New Kings Road
London
SW6 4LY
020 7371 9300
www.thewi.org.uk

Check out what the Shoreditch
Sisters have been up to and
learn how you can join in at:

www.shoreditchsisters.blogspot.com

www.facebook.com/
shoreditchsisterswi

www.twitter.com/londonwi

CRAFTY WEBSITES

www.etsy.com

The online marketplace for
buying and selling all things
handmade and vintage.

www.cutoutandkeep.net

Fun interactive craft site with
masses of step-by-step tutorials
and general inspiration.

www.ravelry.com

Like Facebook but for knitters. Sign
up to swap tips and patterns with
like-minded knitting enthusiasts.

www.knitty.com

A knitting webzine – one of the
best online knitting resources.

www.craftsforcharity.co.uk

Read up on how to put your
crafty skills to good use.

http://craftivism.com

Check out Betsy Greer's
website and blog for more
information on the emerging
Craftivism movement.

http://craftivist-collective.com

Wanna get involved? Well, look
no further than the Craftivist
Collective, who run monthly
meetings, get togethers
and events.

INDEX